From HELLO to YES
in 3 Minutes or LESS

How to Overcome Call Reluctance

Know Exactly What to Say

and Avoid Rejection

When Using the Telephone

as a Network Marketing Professional

By Paul G Walmsley,

www.mytelephonecoachfreeresources.com

Published by Paul G Walmsley.

Form HELLO to YES in 3 Minutes or LESS: How to Overcome Call Reluctance, Know Exactly What to Say and Avoid Rejection When Using the Telephone as a Network Marketing Professional.

For more information about this book and the 30 Day Business Builder for Network Marketing Professionals: Daily Assignments Workbook, along with other helpful tools and resources please visit:

www.mytelephonecoachfreeresources.com

Paul G Walmsley-1st ed.

ISBN-13 978-1497360952
ISBN-10 1497360951
First Edition

Dedicated to my dad, Gordon Walmsley, the most honest, reliable and hardworking man I have ever known. Most of this book was written on my laptop as I sat by his bed from night into the early hours of the morning while he fought his battle with cancer. It was comforting to be there for him in his last few weeks. I love you and miss you, dad.

"Paul Walmsley's coaching came to me at a time when I really needed it. I knew what I was supposed to do, but—HOW? What would I say? Paul's simple phrases and explanations gave me tools to open conversations, to pinpoint follow up times, to overcome objections and more. I am still a student in this wonderful world of network marketing, but I recently earned a free Lexus and I have reached a comfort level now where this business is FUN! And for that I am very grateful to Paul and his teachings."

— Michealle Mitchener

Praise for From HELLO to YES in 3 Minutes or LESS

"You crushed it! I cannot wait to eat this for breakfast, lunch, and dinner and feed this to every single person on my team! You have tangible information and useful strategies that people can implement."

— Juliane Frank

"Amazing job! This book will help a ton of people, who, like me, feel they have no business in sales, believe that they can do it! Every point was easy to understand and follow. Nothing seemed too complicated and appeared to be steps that anyone, no matter their background, could follow."

— Shynasty Wilkes

"Your writing is humble, hilarious, and spot on! Great read and very useful!"

— Sara Nicole

"Paul's support, coaching and tips have been invaluable to me! He has taught me skills that not only serve me now, but that I will carry with me forever. With Paul's training it is much more likely to have the success in this business that everyone is seeking. I am forever grateful!"

— Madie Vilbig-King

"I had one major issue that I had to fix before I could have any type of success with my company—I am an introvert. I had to find a way to get over this hurdle if I wanted to experience any kind of success in my business. I saw Paul Walmsley offering a 30 day accountability group and decided to join. I'm glad I did. Now I can open up genuine conversation with someone I just met without it being weird, share what I do without mentioning anything about my company, the product, or even the compensation plan. Being able to have that type of confidence relieves anxieties and makes it easier to go do my business. I am confident that you could put me anywhere in the USA, with any company that has a decent product or service, and I will be able to build a business. None of this would have been possible without the mentorship and incredible leadership of Paul Walmsley."

— Rajuy Elbey

"I highly recommend this book for any network marketer that wants to advance in this industry. It is full of insights and hands on training and walks you step by step toward your success. I learned more from this man's training in this book than I did in my first two years of network marketing and going to hundreds of training meetings."

— Karen Usevitch

"The first word that comes to my mind about Paul Walmsley is INTEGRITY. He shares his knowledge in an honest and open format that his students can follow and build from."

— Chrissy O'Grady

"Paul Walmsley and his coaching have made a huge impact on my life and the members of my team. He takes the skills required in network marketing and breaks them down into simple, yet challenging baby steps. The manner and skill with which he approaches the subject of telephone work is priceless. I recommend his coaching for anyone—these aren't just entrepreneurial skills, they're life skills. Work with Paul and you'll learn about yourself, gain confidence in yourself and your strengths, and grow by leaps and bounds, thus maximizing your own ability to help others. He'll take you from t-ball to fast pitch in no time. You and your paycheck will thank him!"

— Sascha Stucky

"As a network marketer I've been told over and over to get on the phone and call my list. But until now I just had no idea what to say or how to say it. With Paul Walmsley's formulas it has all become natural and easy and best of all I've learned to "shut the hell up!" I recommend Paul's book to anyone who wants to become better on the phone and take their business to the next level."

— Cherie Leffe Goldsmith

"Taking inventory now, shedding excuses. I can't thank Paul enough for teaching the tools necessary to succeed, for sharing his insight and passion, and for thrusting us in front of the mirror, that is our life, to accept the reality that we choose each and every day if we are willing to do whatever it takes to accomplish our dreams. Thank you, Paul for this invaluable source of direction and encouragement. If you've ever lacked confidence or just needed help being more effective, this detailed guide will quickly become your "go to" resource. Paul is a true mentor, a personal development Jedi Master!"

— Jen Crittendon

Table of Contents

Introduction

This book was written to help network marketing professionals become a little better on the telephone. I am not going to make wild promises of tripling your income if you follow my 3 step secret formula and I am not going to tell you that my book will help you look younger, leaner, meaner, and taller. Using my thirteen years of experience in commission only sales (seven of which were exclusively phone sales) together with my experience entering the world of network marketing, I have been able to identify some common recurring challenges that people have when using the telephone as a network marketing professional. I have made a humble attempt to help people become slightly better on the telephone. No hype, no wild promises, just the nuts and bolts.

The ideas I share in the book are real life, battle tested, proven concepts that work. My challenge has been to present them in a way that they don't come across as "salesy" or as "trickery" or as some kind "sales mumbo jumbo." My goal has been to identify what keeps new and even experienced network marketing professionals up at night and to provide simple, practical, easy to use and duplicatable ideas that may just help.

I start the book off by asking, "What's all the fuss about?" in an attempt to make light of just what we are doing when we pick up the phone to call a friend about an opportunity. I then discuss the phone call itself in relation to where it fits in the duplicatable system employed by network marketing organizations. This is a way of putting the phone call into perspective and taking a little bit of pressure off it. I outline ways to prepare for your phone call session, including providing a useful checklist. Next, I discuss the topic of "call reluctance" which plagues everyone, from the brand new network marketer right through to the seasoned sales pro. I offer some ways to "kick it's ass." Part of the system employed by network marketing companies is to "pique interest" so I outline some tried and tested ways to encourage the person on the other end of the phone to suddenly perk up and pay attention. The prospect, once they have had their interest piqued, then fall back upon common objections or defensive plays and if you are not ready for them, the call is over.

Then I introduce what I call my Simple Success Formula for overcoming all objections. It isn't secret at all, but as the saying goes, "There's nothing wrong with being a copycat, just make sure you copy the right cat." I show you how to use two very powerful words which immediately put your prospect at ease, dropping their defenses instantly. Easing the prospect towards a 3rd Party Tool should be a piece of cake, but often it isn't, unless you employ this very simple three step formula. I caution you to not end a call without doing this powerful thing, or you will kick yourself! Follow up calls are powerful and the meat and gravy of any business. I show you a very simple way of making your follow up calls the best in the business. The use of and the introduction to an expert to talk to your prospect and answer their questions is so key to your success, it is hard to describe. That's why I show you how to edify that expert and how to, with ease, introduce them to your prospect. Then we get to the nitty gritty where I show you a tried and tested way to make the completion of the paperwork and the consummation of the sale a piece of cake. Finally, I throw in three bonus chapters outlining the biggest mistakes and how to avoid them.

Good Luck!

Paul G Walmsley

www.mytelephonecoachfreeresources.com

www.twitter.com/pgwalmsley

https://www.facebook.com/MyTelephoneCoachdotCom

www.linkedin.com/in/pgwalmsley/

Chapter 1
My Story

There was never any plan to be in a position to even attempt to write a book like this. I wasn't supposed to be in sales and I certainly never discussed with my high school careers advisor the lofty heights I could soar to as a telemarketer. No, I was destined to be a pro soccer player or a veterinarian, maybe an agricultural journalist (so that I could write about the newest and baddest tractors). I even flirted with being a fighter pilot until I discovered the joy of puking during almost every training flight (as well as throwing up on the taxiway, much to the horror of Flt Lt Ramage).

As I was rounding out my degree, I confidently applied to all the blue chip companies in the UK, convinced that my CV would have them drooling and clambering over each other to welcome me to the corporate world. Company car, expense account, time on the golf course, business travel, and hot secretary were all part of the plan. Then reality hit and I was moving back in with my parents at 23 years old, tail between my legs with an Honours Degree in agriculture (which my dad and I later unceremoniously dumped into the local tip one day). I answered a very non descript three line ad in the local rag and interviewed with a life insurance company. They showed me just how much money I could make as a commission only salesperson and how much more money I would attract if I worked their Agency Agreement, building a team of fellow studs. All I needed was the ability to fog up a mirror when placed before my face and a list of 50 friends and relatives that I could call to share the joy of paying into something every month and hoping to never receive its spoils.

Mum and dad were gutted. This was not the plan. "So, you mean to say, you could go to work tomorrow and come home not having earned a penny?" Two months into my career I came into the office and my Christmas paycheck was posted on a bulletin board for everyone to see. It amounted to my mum and dad's full time monthly salaries added together and then DOUBLED. Maybe I was on to something. I went on to become Salesperson of the Year for the branch in my first full calendar year. The fancy bottle of champagne I won sat proudly in its display box on my desk as testament. (When I left the company and picked up the box to take it home...yes, you've guessed it, someone had stolen the bottle from inside!)

I then joined another life insurance company and this time it was a "real job" as a sales manager. The company car, pension, expense account and trips had finally arrived. My own office was nice and so was the fried egg butty placed in one hand and a cup of coffee in the other every morning on my arrival. I had made it.

And I was miserable. I had the world's youngest midlife crisis at 26 years old.

This all changed on my 27th birthday when I started a soccer coaching course with a local legend who showed me how to teach other players to do what I had been doing since I could walk. Game changer. This was my ticket out of the humdrum of working a real job. This is what I was going to do forever. So, I made it happen and two years later I was on a plane heading to Squaw Valley, California to coach soccer for 6 weeks with no intention whatsoever of returning to my life of monotony. That 6 weeks turned into 17 years and counting.

I was free. I was in control of my life and I was doing exactly what was written in my DNA. I then spent the next 10 years building up my own soccer business comprised of indoor soccer facilities, retail soccer stores, women's fitness franchises, soccer camps, clinics, tournaments and leagues. All this while having a daughter who preferred my little pony to a soccer ball. At its peak, over 3,000 people per week passed through my business and at its peak I was stressed out and burned out.

When I was approached to be bought out of my business, the business I had devoted 10 years of my life to, it took less than a nanosecond to shake hands. I was free. I was in control of my life again and I had the time to decide exactly what I wanted to do. The following few months were some of the happiest in my life. I ended up coaching the NAIA equivalent of "The Bad News Bears" as I took over a college soccer team the week before the season started. I had started to date an unbelievably hot 26 year old and and life was more than good, it was damn good.

We both decided to reboot our lives and head down to Southern California. My girlfriend's career was all set and I decided I would be a college soccer coach again. However, an NCAA Division III, part time and temporary coaching gig doesn't bring home much bacon. So I looked on craigslist for a job to help boost the family's kitty each week. We only had one car between us, so the criteria for the job was simple: it had to be in such a place that my girlfriend could drop me off in the morning on the way to her real job and pick me up at the end of the day. We decided that if I could earn $500 per week doing this, then cool.

Well, I happened upon the right place at the right time and over the next 5 years this commission only telephone sales job produced an average paycheck of $27,000 per month! As a result I was trapped again. How can you escape from a job that you hate that pays you over $300,000 per year?

I wanted to be free.

I decided to look for a business where I wouldn't have to worry about paying rent, payroll, liability insurance, etc (been there and done that) and that would pay me a residual income for the rest of my life for the work I was going to do initially.

Along came the cult of network marketing.

Once we decided to take the plunge, I knew it was going to be a foregone conclusion that we (girlfriend had turned into wife and mother of my two boys) were going to crush it. After all, I was a sales pro earning multiple six figures a year going up against stay at home moms. Nobody had the sales experience and earnings that I had and I even contemplated going right to the top guy and offering to grace him with my presence as his right hand man.

Then reality hit and I got my ass handed to me.

My earnings in my real job plummeted and I had resigned (for the family) from my soccer coaching passion. Where had it all gone wrong? Due to the fact that my future ex wife and I could not work together in this business like the idyllic couples we had seen at hotel meetings, I handed over the reins of the team we had built and whimpered away with my tail firmly rooted where the sun don't shine. I then watched from the sidelines as people who had no right to do better than me went on to build a residual income in excess of what I was earning in my heyday. I went through a lot of soul searching and tried to find my way.

I set up a soccer coaching blog in an attempt to satisfy my addiction to the game. I even started a sales coaching blog as a ploy to generate sales from one measly ebook. But to no avail. I then undertook some trial and error that would have made Thomas Edison proud. "I haven't failed 10,000 times, I've just discovered 10,000 ways that this thing doesn't work." Thomas Edison, I'm with you.

I met with a dad from my son's school who was an entrepreneur. I described to him how amazing I was at coming up with business ideas, many of them were surefire winners. I even described what I called the "Entrepreneur's Curse" which I proudly had self diagnosed to make me sound like some kind of genius. He called me out right there and then and in no uncertain terms told me that unless I took one idea to market I was no entrepreneur. In fact I was a sad little "shoulda-coulda-woulda kind of guy."

Ouch! And, thank you.

So, the game face was on (all those years as a soccer player and coach were coming back to be useful). I wrestled with how I could combine my passion for coaching with a skill set that would attract paying customers. I also learned that the trick was to find a specific niche and then become the best in the world at that. But what was that niche? Why was it so difficult to find?

Suddenly I had an epiphany (or was it just wind?). Why not find out if difficulty using the telephone was a major hurdle for network marketers and then provide valuable ways to help them? As the saying goes, "He who diagnoses the problem gets paid to provide the solution." So, I recapped my time in network marketing. I then looked at the 300 or so people who had been on my team. I started to facebook message some of my past colleagues and friends and asked them to describe theirs and their team's difficulties. I had diagnosed the problem and I knew that I could provide the solution. I discovered by simply asking all my former network marketing contacts just what their major challenges were when using the telephone in their business, that there were very common themes. The top 3 themes that came back were overcoming call reluctance/fear of using the telephone, knowing exactly what to say when on the phone, and then dealing with rejection when the prospect says no. Here is a list of the most common challenges and concerns I received from my friends on Facebook:

- I have trouble working up the nerve to make calls.
- I am hesitant.
- I don't like the phone at all.
- It feels awkward.
- I want to be more comfortable with calls.
- How do I keep it short and sweet and to the point?
- The phone represents the 600 lb gorilla.
- I struggle with fear of rejection.
- I am frustrated.
- I find myself doing other busy work and not making my calls.
- My biggest fear now is that I will ruin my chances with some very good people who would be perfect.
- I keep looking for the perfect phrase.

- What is the best way to approach them? Because I haven't found it.
- I blew it with many on my top 10 list.
- I have fear over making a call.
- People will think I want something from them.
- I can't pick up the phone.
- I have fear of what people will think. They will want to avoid me like the plague.
- I am terrified of the phone!
- I overthink the conversation.
- I keep focusing on possible objections.
- I have fear of hearing "no."
- They may laugh in my face at the idea of a "pyramid scheme."
- I don't know what to say or how to say it.
- I fear sounding "stupid."
- I fear losing a friend by being too pushy.
- I just can't get into action and pick up that telephone.
- I am embarrassed.
- I am ashamed.
- I don't want people to not like me.
- I can't sell.
- I am not outgoing.
- I fear rejection, I fear failure.
- I fumble around with my words.

- I'm uncomfortable.

- What do I say?

- I quit too soon!

- I'm nervous about getting on the phone.

- I just freeze.

- I'm embarrassed.

- What if they get mad at me?

- What if this changes their opinion of me?

- I fear that people won't answer or they will avoid me and not return my calls.

- I spend too much time with people on the calls.

- I struggle with the issue of the telephone daily.

- I fear hearing someone sound uncomfortable that I called them.

- I have a difficult time keeping my composure.

Now that I had definitely discovered a need for help, I remembered the concept, "he who diagnoses the problem is paid to provide the solution" and I decided to see if I what I had to offer may be of use to my friends. I wrote a simple report and sent it to some of them for their feedback and the comments were very positive. I wrote a proposed chapter of this book and sent that out there and again, the feedback was very positive and helpful. I then recorded a short podcast and let people listen and respond back with their thoughts and again, good things came back to me. I figured that I was on to something and that maybe I could help and maybe there was a business opportunity for me too.

Over the course of the next few months I became very active in Facebook groups and helped in any way I could. I uploaded ten podcasts on iTunes in an attempt to validate again if I had anything useful to offer network marketing professionals and the 5 star reviews came rolling in. ITunes also listed the podcasts as "new and noteworthy". Then people started to ask me when I was going to write this book. I remember one comment in particular: "Write the damn book!"

On January 1, 2014 one of my friends on Facebook messaged me. She had been listening to my podcasts and came to me with a good question. I answered it to the best of my ability and then I asked her if she was really serious and committed this year, and I will never forget her answer: "100%," she said. " I want it more than air." I then offered to work with her one on one for the next 30 days. I couldn't turn down the opportunity to work with someone so committed.

Later that day I threw up a post on Facebook to see if anyone else wanted to work together for the next 30 days in some kind of accountability group. I was blown away by the response! From nowhere, a thriving community of hundreds of network marketing professionals came together and the following month was absolutely amazing. Not only did this group prove to me that there was a need for mentoring, training, and coaching, but it also confirmed to me that I did have something to offer and as a result of the efforts and feedback from the members of the group, this book became a reality.

Here is my vision for this book. I want this book to be in people's purses, on the passenger seat of their car, in their backpack, in their hand. I want this to be a reference book, a game changer, a comfort blankie, and a familiar friend. I hope to see this book covered in notes, emblazoned in highlighter, with corners of pages folded over. I want to see people's books with the cover falling off and its tongue hanging out. My goal is for this book to go everywhere and be that go to guide for network marketing professionals all over the world.

I would love to see photos of you and this book out there in the trenches, partners building your business. Please send them to https://www.facebook.com/MyTelephoneCoachdotCom

Notes

Chapter 2
Why Your WHY is so Important

One of the things that really plagues me in the network marketing industry is the fact that so many people do not make it. So many people quit and that is a massive waste of talent. The industry statistics, from what I can gather, are as follows: for every 20 new distributors who join a company, here is what typically happens:

8 disappear immediately

12 actually do something

8 remain after 90 days

4 remain after 12 months

70% of the total sales volume of the remaining 4 comes from 1 of the 4 distributors

Let's analyze the above. We have all been absolutely flabbergasted by welcoming new distributors onto the team only for them to disappear almost instantly. They go from full of beans, raring to go, to being swallowed up by the network marketing equivalent of the Bermuda Triangle. When this first happened to me I was crushed. I could not figure it out at all. When I discovered the above industry norm, not only did I feel a little more at ease, but it also spurred me on to research why this occurred industry wide and lead me to my third book title (The First 72).

Let's take a look at the 12 that remain. They actually open up their business starter kit and make an attempt at marketing their products and opportunity. They may even experience a little bit of success as their grandma becomes a customer and mom even signs up on the team. One or two co-workers show their support and are a little intrigued by what has gotten into their friend. Then, once they either see their FB page blasted with before and afters, motivational quotes, and photos of complete strangers driving off in brand new cars, coupled with being ambushed by the water cooler or in the restroom, they quickly put up their defenses and put up barriers to ever entertaining their coworkers advances again. As a result, 4 more newly anointed network marketers fall by the wayside.

Now there are 8 remaining and they are in it for the long haul. They have discovered what they were looking for as time, freedom, beach money, and worldwide travel beckons. Initially they have some successes, people who join their team actually get out there and do something. Some weekly checks start to flow and everything is looking rosy. Then the disappointments begin to rack up. No shows, yes's mysteriously switch to no, suddenly people have no time or money and the distributor gets frustrated that the people who really need this, the ones who could really crush it, run to the hills and are never to be seen again. The new distributor then questions themselves, wonders just what they are doing wrong, questions just what is wrong with people nowadays and asks why is it so difficult for them when all the corporate calls, webinars, social media posts and live events are teeming with success after success in record breaking time from people with no previous experience who all sing from the same hymn book with ditties such as "If I can do it, anyone can do it!" and "All I did was plug into the system."

At this stage the next 4 people drop out. At least "they gave it a go" but found out "it wasn't for them." Maybe if they had just joined the company in its infancy then they would sit atop the company structure, raking in the residuals. But they had to start at the bottom and it was much tougher for them, what with the economy and all…

So we are left with the Final Four. These are the ones who stick around for 12 months or more. These are the warriors who put up with the setbacks and are now generating somewhat of a regular monthly income. Three of those four are bringing in enough money to prevent them from quitting, but they just don't have the time or the stomach to go all out and make this a full time career or business. However, the extra couple of thousand a month makes a decent difference to their lifestyle, so they just do enough to maintain their production, show up at the major live events, and are intermittently available to their team.

Finally, the last remaining distributor realizes that this is what they had been looking for. This is the opportunity to leave the cubicle behind, make money while attending parties, build up their income and celebrity status as suddenly their name, title and photo appears on posters and banners for upcoming parties. Not quite rockstars, but as they rank up, not only does their income increase, but so does their billing as they are now being referred to as a "Top Leader" or a "Top Income Earner."

So, let's recap. In the above outline, it is assumed that all the participants worked for the same company, marketing the same products at the same time, in the same economy and in the same location. Let's even assume that they had the same support from their team and company, same training and same socio economic background. So why did 8 quit immediately, only 4 actually "make it" and what was so special about "The One"?

It all comes down to their WHY. Had to be, couldn't be anything else, could it? Of course, "The One" may have gotten lucky and stumbled across a readymade stud, an industry veteran who was ripe and plump, ready to jump ship and bring their entire team with them. Even if that was the case, that is not duplicatable and certainly does not ensure success for the lucky person who falls into this opportunity.

No, I truly believe that new distributors in their first day, week, month, and year are tested so severely that unless they have a cast iron WHY, a WHY so strong that it truly does make them cry, their intestinal fortitude will not be able to cope with setback after setback, disappointment after disappointment, challenge after challenge. Each and every time they build their hopes up only to be let down, they must have a strong enough WHY to fall back on, to climb up upon and rest their weary body so that they can reemerge steely eyed, war paint on, ready to go back out to battle and take on more licks. After all, that's all they have. Products are the same, crazy public is the same, economics are the same.

The people who really get it and have a strong WHY still hurt, they still question, they still ruminate. But they constantly refer to their WHY, be it their kids that they come home to at night, their spouse who is right there with them (or maybe totally against them) or the friend or family member who doubted that they could do this. No matter what it is, their WHY is there, coursing through their veins, bouncing around the double helix of their genome, ricocheting off the inside of their eyelids, constantly there, showing up when needed, spurring them on, consoling them, kicking them in the pants, terrorizing them and playing sweet music in their ears. They can touch it, taste it, feel it, smell it and sense that it is there with them at all times. This is the WHY they have been searching for all their lives. It is why they exist, why they are right here right now, it is what they were meant to do. The thought of not achieving their WHY haunts them and the prospect of successfully satisfying their WHY arouses them, tickles them, makes them giddy, gives them that Christmas morning tingling, that sweaty palm energy, the butterflies in the stomach excitement. They feel like they are pushing the edge of their envelope, they feel alive like Billy Elliot with electricity running through their body. After all, they are bloody well going to need this WHY, because over their first year as a would be network marketing professional, it is about the only thing they can rely upon to get them through those first tough weeks, months, and maybe even years.

Now, if you don't have a WHY such as the one described above, you need to put this book down right here, right now and ask yourself why. This kind of WHY is essential. No, really, you have to have a WHY that is incredibly strong. So, take the time to really assess just why you are attempting to be a network marketing professional. Do you have a WHY that is big enough? Thinking of your WHY right now, just how does it feel? If it is not consuming you as you read, it is not big enough. Go for a walk, talk to your loved ones, dream again, get pissed off with your situation, question just what it is you are doing with your life. Ask how you got to where you are now. Do you know who you are? Do you know where you are going? Do you know how to get there?

You have work to do. Possibly the most important task you have ever set for yourself. But until you can return to this book with your WHY firmly ingrained into every cell of your body, this book will be of no use to you lastingly. Yes, it may give you some neat ideas, some short term motivation, but as soon as the setbacks begin to stack up again, you will be out there searching again for the next shiny object, the next trinket that offers you hope of being a success, the next quick fix formula. Get serious, get real, get on with it and only return when your WHY and your soul are one.

Notes

Chapter 3
Outline the System Used by Network Marketing Professionals

The whole premise of network marketing is that anybody from any walk of life can plug into a proven system, follow that system, and be a success. When promoting the opportunity of joining your network marketing organization, the words that you want your prospect to mutter to themselves are, "I can do that." That's it right there. This is why network marketing systems are so simple and easy to follow. You want your prospect to experience your approach, discover how simple it is, and come to the conclusion that even though they have no prior experience whatsoever, after seeing you in action they realize that you just followed a very simple system that even they could follow.

Network marketing will not work if the person doing the approach presents an amazing A+, in depth performance, covering all aspects of the opportunity from the product through to the compensation plan. Why? Because the person on the receiving end is saying to themselves, "Wow, Carol really knows her stuff. She must have spent a lot of time learning all this and she's always been good at selling. I couldn't do that and I don't have the time to get as good as her either. It's not for me."

Network marketing companies want you to wake up in the middle of the night saying to yourself, "You know what, all Fred did was tell me a little bit about what he is doing, had me watch a video, then introduce me to someone else he works with. I can do that! He didn't even have to answer any of my questions. Wow!"

Now, that's beautiful right there. That's powerful and that is why if carried out correctly the network marketing system of piquing interest, introducing a 3rd Party Tool, following up and using a 3 way call is so powerful. And because it is so simple it is also ripe for abuse and creativity to creep in from people who don't know the simple genius behind it.

Now you know how and why it works and how and why you need to plug into the system. And if you have joined network marketing to build a massive team, you now know why every single one of your team needs to plug into the exact same system, or it will be a nightmare for you and you will fail. Using the telephone in the above system is no different. I am going to show you the system for using the telephone as a network marketing professional.

It is also very important that you plug your entire organization into the exact same system. You want to know that when someone joins your team 8 levels deep and 5 states away from you that they are being plugged into your company's system and the telephone system you will learn here. Then you are really on to something. You are creating leverage and momentum and so long as you

24

monitor and encourage that, you will be set for life.

Let's take a look at a typical system and explain the theory behind it. A typical system involves the distributor approaching a prospect, piquing interest, sharing a 3rd Party Tool, having an expert answer questions, inviting the prospect to a live event if necessary, then signing up the prospect into the team. Once the prospect joins the team, they are plugged into the system and then the whole process is rinsed and repeated.

How does this book fit into the typical system? Well, I believe it pulls it all together and oils the gears of the system. This book is focused on helping network marketing professionals overcome call reluctance, know exactly what to say when on the telephone, and to help them deal with rejection.

The title of the book is *From HELLO to YES in 3 Minutes or LESS*, so what does that mean? *From HELLO to YES in 3 Minutes or LESS* is a system for taking a look at each telephone call, deciding upon the desired outcome of the call (the YES) and then putting together a game plan consisting of proven formulas which will allow the network marketing professional to move from the beginning of the call (the HELLO) through to the desired outcome of the call (the YES) in 3 minutes or less.

Once the desired YES has been achieved, that's the end of the call. The game plan worked and it is important for the network marketing professional to recognize this, end the call and move on to the next call immediately. This book follows a very clear path that involves 4 Mantras, 4 Chords and it all begins with The 5 Second Rule which is explained in Chapter 9.

Notes

_____
_____
_____
_____
_____
_____
_____
_____
_____
_____
_____
_____
_____
_____
_____
_____
_____
_____
_____
_____
_____
_____
_____
_____
_____
_____

Chapter 4
It Doesn't Matter How Good You Are, it Matters What is Duplicatable

As stated in the previous chapter, successful network marketers plug into and follow their company's proven system and then teach their people to do the same. However, many people new to the profession focus on using their existing skills and experience and want to bring all that baggage to the table. I know because I made all the classic mistakes. Being a very successful salesperson, I figured that I could pique interest better than anyone, didn't need to bother with 3rd Party Tools, and certainly didn't need to ask anyone else to come on the telephone call and help me close the deal.

And I failed miserably.

There are many beautiful one liners used in the profession to put the point across that you should follow the system because that is what duplicates. Here are some belters:

"You are the messenger, not the message."

"If your lips are moving, your fingers should be pointing (at a 3rd Party Tool)."

"Dumb it down."

"Never answer your own prospect's questions, let a 3rd Party

Tool or a 3 way call answer them for you."

"3 Way to Pay Day."

The system works because no matter where in the country (or the world), no matter what background or experience the distributor has, if they all follow the same system, they will be successful. You want to know that when someone on your team in Omaha, Nebraska, or Manchester, England is asked, "How do you get paid?" that your team member answers in exactly the same way with either, "I can show you a video which explains our compensation plan," or, "Let me have Jody answer that question for you."

Surely that is much easier than having to train people all over the world on the intricacies of the compensation plan and much more effective when it is presented in such a way that the person asking the question receives the exact same information no matter who, from, or where they are. So, instead of working on yourself, trying to be the best in your company at explaining the compensation plan, or delivering an incredible monologue on the science behind your products, master the art of getting yourself out of the way and employing your company's system. Learn the system, teach the system, and then teach the leaders of your team how to teach the system. That's a successful business model right there.

Notes

Chapter 5
Why is the Telephone so Important?
Can't I Just Text, Tweet, Post or Email?

I honestly believe that many people go to hotel meetings, convention center regionals or nationals, get all fired up and excited about what they see and then sit there and convince themselves that once they join all they will have to do is put a few posts on their Facebook page, send out a few tweets, email some of their contacts, and text some friends. Then they can just sit back, wait for the positive responses, sign up a bunch of people and they will be set for life.

Here's what usually happens in the real world. The new network marketer signs up and immediately gets access to their very own back office. They hunt down the social media collateral such as banners, videos, before and afters, and motivational sayings. Then they log into their respective social media networks and throw up all over them.

There will be an initial response from people over the first couple of days, but unfortunately, the new network marketer will blow it when approaching and responding to those people and within a week or so it's all over. The new network marketer is now down in the dumps because things are turning out to be much more difficult than expected and all of their social media friends are tuning out all the propaganda being spurted out all over the web.

Ouch!

Sorry to break it to you but no, you can't just join a network marketing company and hide behind your laptop or smartphone. You actually have to NETWORK with people and approach them either Belly to Belly or Ear to Ear. This is a home based business and not a homebound business. Sorry to be so brutally honest with you, but you are better off learning this from me right here, right now instead of going through the sorry scenario above...am I right?

There are countless resources on how to use social media effectively to promote your business, so I am not going to go there. What this book will offer is tools to help you when someone responds to a post/tweet/text or email, so long as you do this: respond to their post/text/tweet/email with something like, "Hi Gretchen, thanks for the message, let me have your number and the best time to call and I will be in touch." Then CALL THEM!

Do not answer their questions via text/post/email or tweet. Got it? No really, have you got that? Because if that hasn't registered with you, there's no point reading any more of this book. Just snap the book shut and give it to someone who may just find it useful. Sorry to be so in your face about this, but let's just save you some time if you think that network marketing is just posting on social media. It's not. You must pick up the phone and make the call to get anywhere in this business.

Notes

Chapter 6
Surefire Ways to Overcome Call Reluctance

What is call reluctance and why is it such a big deal? If you remember at the beginning of the book I outlined how I validated the need for this book by asking people in the network marketing profession if they had any challenges when using the telephone in their network marketing business. I then listed the barrage of responses I received from real people that I knew in the profession. To supplement my own "research" I went online and tooled around a bunch of web pages and discovered some interesting facts.

One definition of call reluctance that I found described it as "a career threatening condition (ouch!) which limits what salespeople achieve by emotionally limiting the number of sales calls they make." Now, I hear what you are saying already, "I am not a salesperson, I am not in sales." But yes, you are. You are asking someone to pull out their credit card in exchange for products and/or a business opportunity. Get over it.

Further surfing of the web indicated that the top three reasons people suffered from call reluctance were:

1. Being intimidated by using the telephone.

2. Fear of actually using the telephone.

3. Fear of being pushy.

Other reasons include:

4. Fear of loss of family.

5. Fear of loss of friends.

6. Fear of being unprepared.

7. Fear of humiliation.

Now, go back to the list at the beginning of the book as you see that all the concerns expressed from my friends were in line with the above. So what can we conclude? Well, firstly "suffering from" call reluctance is absolutely normal, whether you are a novice network marketer or a seasoned sales professional. So, the first thing to do is to give yourself a break, go easy on yourself and heave a big sigh of relief knowing that there is nothing wrong with you.

Even for professional phone sales people, call reluctance is the biggest obstacle they have to get over each day. I promise you, myself and all of my colleagues in my regular job sit in front of names of prospects, or even our existing customers, and come up with 101 reasons why we shouldn't call them. And we earn our living on the phone! When a network marketer looks at a list of people to call and then eventually zeros in on a specific person, here are some of the typical excuses they use to convince themselves not to call this one particular person:

- They won't be interested.

- They won't have the time.

- They probably can't afford it right now.

- They've done this kind of thing before.

- They are too successful to want to bother with this.

- What if they get mad at me?

- What if this changes their opinion of me?

Am I jangling any nerves right now? Recognize any of the above? Sure you do and it's OK! Let me present you with some ways to overcome these hurdles:

1. The biggest trick we use in my regular job when facing the daunting prospect of calling someone you are reluctant to call, is to simply share them with a colleague and let them call them for you! BAM! About 60-70% of all the deals I do year after year are shared deals such as this. Either I have shared a person with a colleague and they've called them or vice versa. Why not run through your list and pair up people you are reluctant to call with people in your upline or downline and have them call instead? Then call that person, tell them about your prospect, and then have them call them. I'll offer an example:

"Hi Amber, this is Jenn, you don't know me but I hear you are a good friend of Hilary Jones. (THEN SHUT THE HELL UP.) Well, nothing to worry about, but Hillary did ask me to give you a call, do you have a minute? Great, thanks. Hillary and I are working together on a new project and I asked out of all of her friends, who she thought would crush it at this and she immediately thought of you. Problem is she's terrified to call you about it, nuts eh?" (THEN SHUT THE HELL UP and continue into the call.)

2. In my regular job, if we haven't called a lead within 7 days and have a follow up call scheduled, that lead is taken from us by the company I work for and given to someone else. So, each time you sit down with your buddy, immediately ask them for the list of people they haven't called in the last 7 days and then take them from them! Then give them some of yours. Call theirs and let them call yours. May sound weird, but try it. It is liberating!

3. Tell them your story. There is nothing more powerful than your story. I bet you weren't sitting by your phone, gazing longingly into its screen, counting down the days to when someone close to you called you about a network marketing opportunity! Take a second to just think back and describe to yourself in detail the exact chain of events when you were first approached. Think about your thoughts, your initial reaction, how the call went, what happened next, and how you came to be where you are right now.

What did you think when you were first called about the opportunity with your present company?

_____

_____

_____

_____

_____

What was your first reaction?

_____

_____

_____

_____

_____

What excuses or objections did you have?

_____

_____

_____

_____

_____

What did the person who called you say that convinced you to take
a look at the opportunity?

_____

_____

_____

_____

_____

Now, whatever reaction you receive from the person on the
other end of the line, you can relate to it and deal with it. "I know

Jean, I wasn't expecting a call about _____ when Joe called me. In fact I was kind of pissed off, I thought a screw had come loose in his brain. However, out of respect for Joe I did go to a meeting in Irvine and man was I glad I did!"

4. Review your WHY. As always, before you do anything in this business, review your WHY. Write it down in detail, describe it, picture it, talk to yourself about it, and salivate over it. Then go for it! (We are going to work on your WHY in much greater detail further into the book.)

_____

_____

_____

_____

_____

_____

_____

5. Set expectations. You are not calling your friend to deliver a thesis on the biotechnology behind your company's products and why network marketing is not a pyramid scheme. All you are doing is letting someone know about something you just found out about and asking them if they'd like to know more about it themselves.

6. It's 3 minutes, that's it! Buy an egg timer and use it! Make sure each call lasts no longer than three minutes.

7. Remember, all you are doing is sharing and sorting, not high

pressure selling. You didn't join your company to become a high pressure salesperson, you joined because:

_____

_____

_____

_____

_____

So remember this call is to check in with someone you know and ask them if they'd like to know more, that's it! You are just sorting through everyone and sharing some information with them.

"Hey, the only reason I am calling is that Paul and I have been searching these last couple of years for a way to give us more time with our family and an income that builds up every year. We think we've found it and thought you might want to take a quick look at it too. No pressure, but do you have 10 minutes sometime today to watch a short video? We'd love to see what you think. Maybe we're nuts, so we'd like a second opinion."

8. If your lips are moving, you should be pointing to a 3rd Party Tool.

"Hey Janet, the reason for the call is to simply find 5 minutes so I can drop off a magazine you should take a look at. It's great bathroom reading, but I will need it back. When can we get together? OK, I am on the way."

9. Be honest with them: "You know what, Paddy? I've been trying to pluck up the courage to call you about this for the last couple of days." THEN SHUT THE HELL UP. When they ask what it is or why you needed to pluck up the courage, follow the system of piquing interest.

10. You're just the messenger, not the message. Again, how hard can it be to get someone to confirm their email address so that you can send them a 4 minute video to watch, or to sit down for a few minutes to look at a magazine?

"Hi Joe, I know you are busy, so I'll be quick. If I could drop off a magazine for you, would you read it? Great, only problem is I do need it back on Wednesday, so if that works, I'll drop it off tonight. What's it about? You'll see, I may have lost my mind, let me know when you've read it. See ya."

11. What's the worst thing they could say? "Don't call me again." Or even worse, "I wish you had called me last week. I'm going to a home party tonight with a girl from work who is with your company already." Need I say more?

12. Buddy up with someone. There's nothing better than being in the trenches with someone. TEAMWORK MAKES THE DREAMWORK. Meet at your local hang out for 30 minutes for the sole reason of calling 10 people on your list. No other reason. Then go back to your regular life.

13. Make it short and sweet, no big deal. Again, the call is only

going to be 3 minutes maximum and you are going to rush through your calls as quickly as possible.

"Hey Angie, sorry I sound so rushed but I need to send you an email. What's your address? What's it about? You'll see, but if I send you a link to my website you'll find 4 minutes to watch this video, won't you? Thanks. By the way, you might think I have lost my mind, but I'll explain later. See ya!"

14. Remember, someone else could be planning on calling them today. Need I say more?

15. Practice and prepare. The more confident you are, the more likely you are to make the calls. Confidence comes from having practiced and prepared, just like in other parts of your life.

16. Make it as light hearted as possible.

"Hey, no big deal, but I have a magazine to drop off for you. It's called------ and there is something in there I want you to look at. Only problem is, I need to get it back from you by Thursday. I have a bunch of people waiting for it."

17. Are they above you or below you? Choose an appropriate strategy. If below you, be direct: "You need to come to a little get together I am having next Wednesday. Trust me on this one, I thought of you right away. No excuses, you'll be there, right? If above you: "Can you do me a favor? I need your opinion. I just joined a new company and I don't know if I've made a mistake.

Can you take a look at it for me?"

18. Remember the SW Rule: some will, some won't, so what? There's always someone else waiting....next!

Notes

Chapter 7
The 4 Mantras

The whole basis of my training and coaching is centered around 4 mantras. Let's discuss them.

Mantra 1: You must have a game plan for every telephone call you are going to make.

From my years as a soccer player and soccer coach, as well as my very brief tenure in the Royal Air Force, I have learned the importance of having a game plan and being prepared and ready. I would never consider sending out a team of NCAA soccer players into battle without a game plan. I would never jump in the cockpit of an aircraft without being fully aware of and prepared for all and every possible emergency.

So, why would I pick up the telephone with the opportunity to speak to someone who could earn me millions over the coming years (all narcissistic of me I know) without being prepared and having a game plan? I wouldn't and I don't, but do you? From now on, before you pick up the telephone, take some time to put together a game plan for that particular person and that particular call. Run through all the things that could go well and all the things that could go not so well and have plans in place to deal with all outcomes.

Don't try to wing it, don't fly by the seat of your pants or you may as well "Buy the farm" as Chuck Yeager said in his fascinating book *The Right Stuff.*

Mantra 2: From HELLO to YES in 3 Minutes or LESS

Let me explain again what I mean by From HELLO to YES in 3 Minutes or LESS. All too often people with little or no experience in network marketing pick up the telephone once they have made their list and immediately call the hottest prospects they think they have. They then spend the next 30-60 minutes throwing up all over those prospects, telling them all about the company, the products, the compensation plan, the parties, the big earners, and how this company is not running a pyramid scheme.

As the person on the other end of the line begins to become cooler and cooler, the inexperienced person thinks that the solution is to throw more information at them hoping that something will do the trick. At the end of the new network marketer's first night on the telephone, they have completed only 3 calls, none of which went anywhere near according to plan. They are exhausted, demotivated and frankly scared to death and wondering if they made the right decision to take up this opportunity in the first place. Two more telephone sessions like that and they are out of the business.

With our second mantra, From HELLO to YES in 3 Minutes or LESS, the whole premise is firstly, and no rocket science here, to keep the phone call down to 3 minutes or less. To do this we use an egg timer on the desk and a whole boatload of discipline, especially at first. Next, we work backwards from the Yes that is desired, put together and practice a game plan, and develop the Hello part of the call at the beginning and how to take the temperature of the person on the other end of the line. And that's it! To recap:

- Define the YES you are aiming for.
- Work backwards with a game plan towards it.
- Figure out your HELLO and take their temperature.
- Set the egg timer.
- Pick up the telephone.

Let's look at some of the possible YES'S to aim for:
- YES, you can send me an email with some information.
- YES, I will check out your website.
- YES, you can stop by with a magazine.
- YES, I will listen to a CD tomorrow on my way to work.
- YES, I will meet you for coffee and watch a video on your iPAD.
- YES, I will come to your party next week.

- YES, I would like to try the products for a few days.
- YES, I will come to the event with you.
- YES, I want to become a customer.
- YES, I want to join your team!

Remember, we start with the desired YES and work backwards. We start the call and as soon as the desired YES has been accomplished, we confirm it and then we get off the telephone. How do we keep the telephone call down to 3 Minutes or Less? As mentioned earlier, we employ the use of an egg timer and then we adopt the discipline of a sniper. We focus on the egg timer and we concentrate on not going over the 3 minutes. It will be tough at first, no question. But once you master this discipline it will be liberating. All you will want to do is shout from the rooftops as you feel amazingly powerful and confident that you can knock out any telephone call in 3 minutes or less.

Mantra 3: THEN SHUT THE HELL UP

In my regular sales job, my catchphrase throughout all of the training I have delivered over the years, the people I have helped earn hundreds of thousands of dollars a year in commissions has been: THEN SHUT THE HELL UP. You will already have heard the term, "the silent close" and maybe even "He who speaks first loses." Although they do sound salesy and cheesy, they are very effective and I use silence in all walks of life. It is incredible how powerful silence can be. This will be one of the toughest parts of this whole system to master, but once you do you will be blown away by how effective it is.

It is very important to ask good questions and then LISTEN for the answer. You see, once you go silent, listen and really tune in to exactly what the person on the other end of the line is revealing, then you gather crucial information and can formulate your game plan and responses. You must stay quiet even once the initial response seems to be completed, because often there are still some gems of information waiting to be revealed if you only keep quiet and let the other person spill the beans.

Throughout this book and in all of my training, you will learn to ask a good question, or tell a good story, and THEN SHUT THE HELL UP. Not just for the sake of it, but for the specific reason of allowing and encouraging the person on the other end of the line to open up and really let the cat out of the bag. While you are being silent, be sure to really listen to your prospect and take notes so that you have all of the information you need.

Mantra 4: Use a Formula

In one of my previous lives I had the privilege of joining the Royal Air Force Volunteer Reserves when I was a student at Aberdeen University in Scotland. I was fortunate enough to be taught how to fly an aircraft by arguably the finest air force in the world. In a typical 60 minute training flight, we would be subjected to 3-4 different simulated emergencies so that I would be ready in case a real emergency happened and it was literally a life or death situation.

In my flight suit, in a pocket, on my right thigh was my flight reference cards, which were made up of a checklist of all the procedures involved in flying the aircraft. Part of these flight reference cards contained all the emergency drills. So, in theory, if I had an emergency to deal with I could quickly whip out the FRCs and read through what I needed to do. Problem was, if I had the aircraft upside down in the middle of practicing my aerobatics, and I was hit with an emergency, it would be difficult to be messing around, digging into my pocket, and flipping to the correct page to figure out what to do! So, instead we had to memorize all of the procedures and checks so that I instantly knew what to do in any eventuality.

For example, I can still remember the procedure for a non-mechanical engine failure: Fuel-Ignition-Induction Air-Mixture-RPM-Throttle. So, if I was presented with such an emergency I could immediately run through the above checks and hopefully discover and rectify the problem. Remember, by this time I could be upside down, spinning toward planet Earth, not much time to think, life and death scenario. That's why every single time I flew with an instructor I was subjected to at least 3 emergency drills. It was exhausting, stressful, but necessary to save my life and prove that I was ready to progress to the next stage of my training.

Fortunately, making little old telephone calls for your network marketing business is not as death defying as flying aerobatics, but you get my drift? If the person on the other end of the telephone throws you an emergency (objection) to deal with, wouldn't it be handy to have the exact procedure to follow memorized, practiced, and second nature at your disposal? This is why I break everything down into formulas for you so that you can have your own readymade set of flight reference cards available. Yes, you can refer to them but better to memorize and master them, don't you think?

Notes

_____

_____

_____

_____

_____

_____

_____

_____

_____

_____

_____

_____

_____

_____

_____

_____

_____

_____

_____

_____

_____

_____

Chapter 8
The 4 Chords

I recently went to a marketing seminar (I am kind of a junkie for these) in Del Mar California and the organizer played us a youtube video called The Four Chords by a group in New Zealand. The video had 29 million hits the last time I took a look. The gist of the video is that pretty much every hit song from the last 50 years has been written using the same four chords. In fact, if you master those four chords, you can play any of those songs easily.

So, it got me to thinking. What if a musician knew that fact but decided to change one of those chords because they didn't like playing that chord and preferred another one instead? How would those very same tunes sound? What if a musician decided to totally omit one of the chords altogether because they didn't like using that chord or had never took the time to learn it? How bad would that sound?

See where I'm going with this? What if a network marketing professional knew that there were four techniques (chords) to master when using the telephone in their business but they decided to change one of those because they didn't like doing it and prefered another technique (chord) instead? What if a network marketing professional decided to totally omit one of the techniques (chords) altogether because they didn't like using it or didn't think it was necessary? How bad would their "performance" be? Have I struck a chord? (Forgive the pun.)

Hopefully this analogy works to help you realize that by coming up with a different "chord" or missing out on one altogether that the "tune" you are attempting to play would sound really terrible. Let's look at The 4 Chords when making telephone calls in the network marketing profession:

Chord1: Piquing Interest

Chord 2: Introduction of a 3rd Party Tool

Chord 3: The 3 Way Call

Chord 4: Asking for the Order

Keeping the analogy going, what kind of tune would you play if you decided that you would not use a 3rd Party Tool but wanted to explain the opportunity to your prospect instead? What kind of tune would you play if you decided to omit 3 way calls from your performance completely?

Exactly.

So, wouldn't it make sense to take the time, put in the effort, and discipline yourself to learn and master all of the above 4 chords and use them correctly for every performance? Sweet music to your ears! In the following pages we will focus on mastering the 4 chords. But before we do so, we need to employ The 5 Second

Rule.

Notes

Chapter 9
The 5 Second Rule

This is a game changer, so let's describe it right away. When you are out and about and you identify a potential prospect for your business or product, or when you are staring at your prospect list with your telephone in hand, The 5 Second Rule kicks in. During that 5 seconds your mind comes up with reasons why you should and should not approach or call that person. By the end of the 5 seconds your mind is made up one way or the other. There is no going back. That's The 5 Second Rule.

Let's step into your mind when this situation arises. You are in your office or local hang out with the sole intention of making telephone calls to your list. You get yourself all situated with your usual beverage, maybe a snack, your planner, tablet, maybe a motivational book or trinket and then you pull out your list, ready to mount a telephone campaign that could go down in history. You start at the top of the list and there he is sitting full of pomp and circumstance, proudly at the pinnacle of your entire business: Adolfo. Then The 5 Second Rule kicks in.

No, (you think to yourself) *this is not for Adolfo. He just graduated college, started his first real job, and spends all of his free time with his girlfriend.*

Or,

Yes, I will call Adolfo. He just graduated college and started his first real job. I bet he doesn't get the personal development training that we provide and I am sure he would love an additional income stream to help him pay off his student loans. Even better, he hangs out with his girlfriend all the time, she knows a ton of people and maybe she'd be up for looking at this as well!

Same prospect, same set of circumstances and two very different outcomes in just a 5 second time frame. Similar thing happens 20 times a day as you go about your business. I know you have countless examples of times where you have noticed someone and during the following 5 seconds you talked yourself out of approaching them. Then, you sheepishly meander out to your car trying to justify why you blew it and then have that heavy feeling in the pit of your stomach when you realize what an opportunity you have just walked away from.

If you have worked on your WHY and have confidence in it, if it wildly motivates you and you find yourself in front of someone you would like to approach or call, as you recognize The 5 Second Rule kicking in, don't hesitate! Do the right thing. Don't talk yourself out of it, don't shrink away from the opportunity. Rather, be brave and make the telephone call!

Notes

Chapter 10
Open Up a Conversation and Build Rapport Using FORM

When opening up a conversation with a prospect either on the telephone or Belly to Belly, it is important to use a formula so that you have a track to run on. This avoids awkward silences, improves your confidence level, and presents you with the opportunity to pick up a ton of valuable information. Also, it is very important that you connect with your prospect emotionally, otherwise all the logic in the world is not going to be enough to have them take the desired action you want.

A fundamental tenet in marketing is that people need to KNOW, LIKE and TRUST you before they will do business with you. This simple formula goes a long way to make that happen:

FAMILY

OCCUPATION

RECREATION

MOTIVATION

When striking up a conversation, especially over the telephone, it is so important to engage the prospect immediately and have them start talking and opening up to you. So, using the

61

above formula, once you have got the formalities out of the way, make sure you touch on each one of the above categories using simple questions such as:

"So, how's the family?" Or, "What have the kids been up to lately?" (FAMILY)

"How's work going?" Or, "Anything new going on at work?" (OCCUPATION)

"What fun plans do you have for the weekend?" Or, "What kind of things do you do at the weekend?" (RECREATION)

"How's things? How are you feeling?" (MOTIVATION)

Now, when they start to answer those questions SHUT THE HELL UP and LISTEN intently. Show real interest, express real concern as necessary. Don't blow off their answers while thinking of your next question. By now your prospect is moving closer to you, feeling more comfortable, and you have all the necessary intel to move on to our next formula which is discussed in Chapter 12: problem identify, problem agitate, problem solve.

Notes

Chapter 11
Mastering Chord 1: How to Pique Interest

Now that we know just what the 4 chords are for using the telephone in your network marketing business and we know the importance of mastering each one of them, let's work on each individual chord and perfect it. Let's first of all define what the heck we mean by "pique interest."

Origin of Pique:

French piquer, literally, to prick

First Known Use: 1669

Definition of PIQUE from Merriam-Webster Dictionary:

1: to arouse anger or resentment in: irritate

2. a: to excite or arouse especially by a provocation, challenge, or rebuff

   b: pride

Wow, fascinating stuff! A fine balance between exciting someone and pissing them off! That's the challenge we all face right there in a nutshell! So, in our terms, we certainly don't want to arouse anger or resentment, irritate or offend. Instead, we want to excite someone to take action, to stimulate a feeling or emotion and awaken their interest. Sounds like a lot, doesn't it? Especially since we only have 3 minutes to do it in! Let's break it down and keep it real simple. My definition of piquing interest is to cause the person on the other end of the line to prick (pique) their ears up and say: "Huh?" followed by, "What?" and then, "I want to know more."

A great way to visualize this is to picture a dog when its interest has been piqued. What does it do? Its ears perk up, its eyes widen and it tilts its head to one side. That's exactly what you want the person on the other end of the telephone to do! That's it! Once they wake themselves up out of their slumber with a "Huh?" followed by a "What did he just say?" and a "What was that?" their interest has well and truly been piqued. So, how do we cause the prospect to ask themselves any or all of the above questions? We pique their interest by opening up with our WHY.

How to Pique Interest by Opening with Your WHY

I recently attended the Network Marketing Pro Recruiting Mastery Event in Las Vegas and the host, Eric Worre, began the four day event by having us watch a TEDX Talk from Simon Sinek in which he described "The Golden Circle." Simon has written the book *Start With Why* and I devoured it after my interest had been piqued by the 17 minute video clip we watched. Simon's findings state that successful leaders and organizations start with their WHY first, then describe HOW they achieve their WHAT.

Most people and companies do it the other way around, beginning with their WHAT, describing their HOW and then explaining WHY.This is far less powerful than the previous method. When asked at a coffee shop or on the telephone, "What do you do?" most network marketing professionals describe what they do, then go into how they do it and then finally they may reveal why they do it. BORING and uninspiring. They lost the person at WHAT when they could have deeply aroused their interest with WHY.

The WHY is nothing new in network marketing. It means to answer why you joined the company and why network marketing is for you. Companies that provide some sort of plan or roadmap for new distributors will usually have space to jot down the new team member's WHY. A few lines. Not much fuss. Never giving the WHY the actual respect it deserves even though the saying, "If your WHY doesn't make you cry then it's not big enough" is one of those network marketing sayings carved in a stone tablet somewhere.

I understand the power of WHY and so when I started my first 30 Day Accountability Group on Facebook, the very first assignment was to watch Simon Sinek's TEDX Talk and then have the group members work on their WHY. I had no idea this was going to have such a profound effect on members of the group. It took on a life of its own and for some, this exercise was truly a life changing experience. I had people posting their WHY on the group page, messaging me, calling me, emailing me, all asking if I could review and refine their WHY. We had people posting selfie videos on the group page describing their WHY in tears, emotions really flooding out. I felt humbled and a little bit intimidated about how this really struck a chord with people. I knew that the WHY was powerful but this experience really solidified it for me.

As this powerful tool has developed, it has morphed into two different WHYS: the deeply personal WHY and the interest piquing WHY. The first WHY is the one that resonates right to your core, is part of your DNA, the reason for being. I encourage people to really take a deep look inside themselves and peel back as many layers as possible. This WHY will be referred to when a setback shows up, a disappointment appears, or a challenge is presented. This is the WHY that waits for you in the morning as you wake up and contemplate getting out of bed. This is the WHY that inspires you to leap out of bed and hit the ground running!

One of the common mistakes people make when delivering this first WHY is describing their WHAT instead of their WHY. For example: "I want to be debt free" is a what, not a why. Why do you want to be debt free? How would that make you feel. How would you go about your day differently? How would that affect your goals and dreams? Why is being debt free so important to you? What has stopped you from being debt free so far? These are the sort of questions you need to ask yourself when generating your WHY. Dig deeper.

Another major mistake people make when describing their WHY is that it is too general, too wishy washy and sounds like a Miss Universe speech. For example: "I want to help homeless people, save the rainforests, mentor kids from inner cities, etc." All worthy causes. All whats and no whys. Dig deeper. Get to the real core reason for why you want to do this. When your true WHY is revealed I am sure it will have a profound affect on you as it has on so many others that I have coached. It will be the engine behind all that you do.

Once you have the personal WHY down, it is time to come up with a 30 second INTEREST PIQUING WHY. This is the WHY that is delivered over the telephone, in a coffee shop, in line at the grocery store, on the bleachers at your kid's softball game, and wherever else you find yourself in front of another person you would like to approach with this opportunity. This is the WHY, that when delivered, should stop your recipient in their tracks. You want to nail them right between the eyes, to jolt them out of their slumber. You want the WHY to haunt the recipient for the rest of the day, to influence them so profoundly that they cannot get you and your WHY out of their head. You want the recipient to sit up and say to themselves, "I want to be a part of that. I want to be led by this person. I want a piece of this."

I suggest you put your WHY on the back of your business card with the introduction: "Before I explain what I do and how I do it, let me explain WHY I do what I do." Man, does that work a treat! Go on, work on this, have fun with it, practice and perfect it. It will not only add a whole new dimension to your work but it will blow away your recipient, giving them the most impactful 30 seconds of their lives. Again, we want to pique your prospect's interest so that they ask you what you do. Achieve this by telling them WHY you do what you do and set yourself apart from the crowd.

Notes

Chapter 12
Problem Identify, Problem Agitate, Problem Solve

Full disclosure here, just being a copycat again. I learned this formula one morning driving to work listening to a CD from marketing legend Dan Kennedy:

Problem Identify

Problem Agitate

Problem Solve

We remember that he/she who diagnoses the problem gets paid to provide the solution. In any sales training you are taught that people are motivated to buy things or take action due to one of two reasons: Greed or Fear of Loss, with the latter being the most powerful. Your job is to identify a problem that your prospect may be experiencing, have your prospect describe their problem in more detail (agitate it), then pique their interest by introducing a potential solution to their problem.

Let's take greed first. What kinds of things would people like to add to their lives and lifestyle? What are they "greedy" for?

- More money
- More time

- Better vacations
- Nicer car
- Nicer house
- Better education for their kids
- The latest toys
- Fancier clothes

What are the things people fear losing?

- Losing their time
- Losing their freedom
- Losing their ability to make choices
- Missing out on experiences with their loved ones
- Losing their ability to pay the bills
- Losing their savings and investments
- Losing their retirement funds and opportunities
- Losing their self worth
- Losing their self confidence
- Losing their passion
- Losing their zest for life
- Losing their optimism
- Losing their dreams

Before you dive into the telephone call with your prospect, you have to have a game plan. Are you going to identify a Greed Problem or a Fear of Loss Problem? Remember, which ones are more powerful? The ones from the Greed list or the ones from the Fear of Loss list? Here is an example. Let's say you are wanting to call a friend of yours who has a couple of toddlers, a husband and now has to go back to work to help contribute to the family finances. Sure, she enjoys her career, but what kinds of problems could she have? Go on and list them here:

_____

_____

_____

So, maybe the three minute conversation (From HELLO to YES in 3 Minutes or LESS) could be used to have her bring up her problem (problem identify), describe it to you in detail (problem agitate) and then you pique her interest by offering a potential solution to her problem (problem solve).

"Hi Jody, Sally here. How's it going?"

"Cool, how's the family?" (FAMILY)

"And work?" (OCCUPATION)

"What's going on this weekend?" (RECREATION)

"And how are you feeling?" (MOTIVATION)

Now, you may need all four of the above, you may just need one of them to identify a potential problem. Once you think you've identified a problem, don't dive in right away with your solution, have them agitate the problem a little more.

"Sorry to hear you are not getting enough time with the boys, what did you miss recently?"(FAMILY)

"I know, it sucks when your boss is a nightmare, what's his latest trick?" (OCCUPATION)

"Oh, I thought you guys were going to go camping this weekend, what happened?" (RECREATION)

"I don't like to hear you sound so down in the dumps, what's going on?" (MOTIVATION)

Once your prospect has identified her own problem, described it in detail (agitated it), you are now ready to pique her interest with a potential solution.

"I hear you, Bill and I have been looking for a way to generate an extra income so that I can be home more to spend time with the kids, we think we've found it with (your company and/or products)." (FAMILY)

THEN SHUT THE HELL UP.

"I know, I used to have a boss that was a nightmare too, that's why I've been looking high and low for a way to one day fire my boss and thanks to (your company and/or products) I think I've found it." (OCCUPATION)

THEN SHUT THE HELL UP.

"Jessica and I decided that weekends were going to be the time we would have fun with the family, trying out new hobbies and sports. (Your company and/or products) has given us the opportunity to do that." (RECREATION)

THEN SHUT THE HELL UP.

"You know what, I was sick and tired of being sick and tired so I decided to do something about it and along came (our company and/or products)." (MOTIVATION)

THEN SHUT THE HELL UP.

Now, I have given examples above where you drop in your company name and/or product(s). Another way of piquing interest (it requires more discipline, but in my opinion it is much more powerful), is to avoid using your company name or product line. For example:

"I hear you. Bill and I have been looking for a way to generate an extra income so that I can be home more to spend time with the kids and we think we've found it." (FAMILY)

THEN SHUT THE HELL UP.

"I know, I used to have a boss that was a nightmare too, that's why I've been looking high and low for a way to one day fire my boss and I think I've finally found it." (OCCUPATION)

THEN SHUT THE HELL UP.

"Jessica and I decided that weekends were going to be the time we would have fun with the family trying out new hobbies and sports. Then this opportunity came along and now we have taken up..." (RECREATION)

THEN SHUT THE HELL UP.

"You know what, I was sick and tired of being sick and tired so I decided to do something about it and along came this opportunity and I've never looked back." (MOTIVATION)

THEN SHUT THE HELL UP.

Be a professional and test different approaches to pique interest. Assess which ones work the best, find out if dropping in your company name or product line works better, or if leaving them with a cliffhanger where they ask you about the opportunity works better. There is no right or wrong answer, figure it out then run with it and perfect it.

Remember my definition of piquing interest? My definition of piquing interest is to cause the person on the other end of the line to prick (pique) their ears up and say: "Huh?" followed by "What?" and then "I want to know some more."

They are either going to physically speak the above words so that you hear them, or they are going to say them to themselves. It's your challenge to figure out just where they are in all of this because what happens next is that their defensive mechanism kicks in and asks the following questions:

"What are you trying to sell me?"

"How much does it cost?"

"What's in it for me?"

"Why should I trust you?"

Remember one of the sacred tenets of network marketing: you never answer your own prospect's questions This is when you need the self discipline of a ninja because as soon as your prospect asks a good question, it is the defining moment of the telephone call, the watershed, the be all and end all of the call.

You are either going to get your game face on and follow the system, or you are going to blow it big time and throw up all over your prospect. Your choice, over to you, simple as that. So when your prospect signifies that their interest has been piqued by asking a good question, all you need to do then is breathe, recognize the opportunity to move into the next part of the system and introduce a 3rd Party Tool.

Notes

Chapter 13
Mastering Chord 2: How to Introduce a 3rd Party Tool

Remember, this second mantra, Introducing a 3rd Party Tool is still part of your original 3 minute phone call. The first part of the call was to pique interest and the second part of the call is to satisfy that interest with the use of a 3rd Party Tool. The YES in this call is, "YES, I will watch the video" etc.

Now that your prospect's interest has been well and truly piqued, it is time to be disciplined and follow the system and introduce your 3rd Party Tool. Before you make the call you create a game plan, remember? Part of the game plan is to have already chosen the 3rd Party Tool you want to introduce, maybe have another one as a backup too in case it is needed. This is huge, it is so important that you introduce the 3rd Party Tool correctly so that the prospect associates some value to it and is motivated to actually watch/listen/read/experience it. Here is how you do it:

"Great question _____ AND THAT'S WHY YOU NEED TO...."

- Watch a video I am going to email you

79

- Read the magazine I am going to drop off
- Meet me for coffee tomorrow and watch a video on my iPad
- Come with me to a little party we are having on Thursday
- Hang out with me on Saturday morning at a big event we are putting on
- Experience this product for yourself
- Listen to the CD I am going to drop off tonight when you are driving to work in the morning
- Check out my website

You tee up the 3rd Party Tool with the formula "Great question, AND THAT'S WHY YOU NEED TO...."

"Great question Julie, and that's why you need to read the magazine I have for you."

Then you button down the use of the 3rd Party Tool, add value to it, and set up the follow up. Here's the formula to use:

"If I COULD, WOULD you, and WHEN can I? BECAUSE..."

"If I COULD stop by tonight with a magazine, WOULD you read it, and WHEN can I pick it back up, BECAUSE I have other people waiting for it."

BAM!

"IF I COULD send you a link to my website, WOULD you

check it out for a few minutes? And WHEN can I circle back to see what you liked? BECAUSE this is big and I don't want you to be left behind."

"If I COULD meet with you and buy you a coffee, WOULD you watch a short video on my iPad? And WHEN can we get together? BECAUSE my diary is filling up fast, this thing is crazy."

So, we actually used two formulas together there, let's recap:

"Great question _____ AND THAT'S WHY YOU NEED TO..."

Then you introduce the idea of a 3rd Party Tool:

"Great question Angie, AND THAT'S WHY YOU NEED TO read the magazine I have for you..."

Then we wrap it up and button it down with:

"If I COULD...WOULD YOU? WHEN CAN I? BECAUSE..."

"If I COULD stop by with the magazine, WOULD YOU read it? Great! And WHEN CAN I circle back with you to pick it up BECAUSE I have other people waiting to get their hands on it."

Let's put the two together:

"Great question Angie, AND THAT'S WHY YOU NEED TO read the magazine I have for you. If I COULD stop by with the magazine tonight, WOULD YOU read it? Great! And WHEN

CAN I circle back with you to pick it up BECAUSE I have other people waiting to get their hands on it."

As soon as your prospect agrees to have you come over with the magazine that is your YES achieved, wrap up the call and get off the telephone. Do not start to ramble on about anything to do with the company, the opportunity, the products, testimonials, etc. You've successfully gone "From HELLO to YES in 3 Minutes or LESS" so say goodbye. No, really, get off the telephone!

If, instead of agreeing to your offer of the magazine to read, the prospect has some kind of wishy washy, laid back kind of response such as:

"Well, I guess I can take a look at it if I have time." Or, "I am super busy, I'll try to get to it." You need to pull back, re-agitate their problem and make them want to watch the video.

"You know what Julie, maybe this isn't for you. The magazine is full of people just like us who have taken control of their lives and are grabbing back some time for their families (or whatever the prospect's problem is). Surely it is worth taking a look. I am real glad I took the time, an extra 5 paychecks a month certainly helps."

THEN SHUT THE HELL UP.

When they come back with: "No, you're right I will take a look at it, it sounds interesting."

You respond with: "Are you sure? I don't want you to feel

pressured in any way, but this might just be what you need, could be a whole new lease on life."

THEN SHUT THE HELL UP.

You are done, Chords 1 and 2 played to perfection! By the way, let's set up the 3 way call perfectly before you even follow up.

"Oh, yes Julie, I almost forgot, when I come to pick up the magazine once you've read it, you'll no doubt have some good questions so I'll try and make sure Amber is available, she's great, she answered all of my questions when I first read the magazine."

Oh mama, freakin' genius! But wait! There's more! What if I could show you a way to double or triple your number of prospects before you hang up the telephone? What if I could share with you a little one liner that not only doubles or triples your number of prospects, but also makes a significant step towards having your prospect join your organization? Ready? Before you hang up the telephone, let this puppy out of the bag:

"Oh, by the way Julie, when I stop by tomorrow with the magazine....WHO ELSE SHOULD WE GIVE ONE TO?"

Or,

"Oh, by the way Julie, when we meet for coffee tomorrow, WHO ELSE SHOULD WE INVITE?"

Or,

"Oh, by the way Julie, when I get back to my office later and send you the email, WHO ELSE SHOULD WE SEND IT TO?"

By asking this absolutely priceless question, you have not only doubled or tripled your number of prospects, but as soon as Julie comes up with a name or two, she is already, almost on board! She has switched her mindset from being a little defensive to thinking of who else she could share this with. That is a massive step forward! You're welcome!

Notes

Chapter 14
Mastering Chord 3: How To Follow Up and Set Up a 3 Way Call

Now everything is going to plan and the system is working to a tee. You've piqued interest by identifying a problem, agitated it a little, and then offered a potential solution. When your prospect asked a question about what you were talking about, you exhibited restraint and you introduced a 3rd Party Tool. You then scheduled a follow up and indicated that you may also have someone else available to answer any questions.

Now is the time to make that follow up call. But guess what? You need a game plan! Firstly, by following our second mantra of "From HELLO to YES in 3 Minutes or LESS" you need to establish just what your desired YES is going to be. In this telephone call the desired YES is going to be "YES I would like to speak to _____." And that's it!

Now you need to work backwards from the desired YES, figure out which FORMULAS to use, when to use "THEN SHUT THE HELL UP and wrap this all up in your GAME PLAN.

See how this is all coming together?

Ask yourself who you want to carry out the 3 way call and

why? What do you want them to achieve on the call? Do you have or need any more 3rd Party Tools available if the expert suggests they may be needed? Before you make the call, make sure your expert is aware and is going to be available.

When you make the call and start with the HELLO, it is important that you take your prospect's temperature right away. I always take their temperature like this:

"Hello Julie, this is Paul from (your company). I dropped off the magazine on Tuesday." THEN SHUT THE HELL UP. And listen for the warmth of their response.

"Oh, hi Paul! Man, I was up all night, couldn't sleep, that magazine blew me away. What happens next? How do I get on board?"

Or,

"Oh, right, you said you were going to call."

Can you feel the temperature difference between those two responses? I bet you can! It is important that you take the time to take their temperature so that you know exactly what you need to do next with the call. If you get a super warm response like the first one then get the application form out and sign them up without any further discussion (more on that with Chord 4). If you sense a colder temperature, you need to know immediately what to do to try and warm them up or put them out of their misery.

Guess what? You need a game plan! Be prepared for the hottest of all responses and have your application form ready and know it inside out and back to front, so that as soon as they indicate they are ready, you are too and in less than 3 minutes you will have made a sale.

Your game plan needs to include responses for all manner of temperatures from pretty warm right through to ice cold. Let's take a look at a few possibilities. You are hoping for a super hot response, but that doesn't happen often, so realistically you want a response with this kind of temperature:

"Oh hi Paul, thanks for following up. That magazine was pretty interesting, I enjoyed reading it. Don't know if it's for me, but I am glad I took a look at it."

Here's your response: "Hey, that's great Sue, I loved the part about...what did you like the best?"

THEN SHUT THE HELL Up. No please, really, really keep quiet and let her talk. When you think she has finished, throw this belter in:

"That's cool...ANYTHING ELSE?...

THEN SHUT THE HELL UP. This little gem of a question might just open up Pandora's Box and unearth the pearl you were hoping for.

"Well, I did like reading about Debbie and Bill, I could really relate to them, they seemed like real people having fun together."

BINGO!

"ME TOO! That's why we should see if Amber is available. She may be able to tell you more about them, I am sure she's met them. Hold on, let me get her on the line."

HALLELUJAH.

There's the formula for your 3 way call. What do you mean you missed it? Here it is again:.

"ME TOO and THAT'S WHY...we should see if _____ is available."

Now, can't you see why bringing Amber up when you dropped off your 3rd Party Tool was a stroke of genius? I know, you can thank me later. But before we get Amber on the line, let's EDIFY her correctly. Here we go with the dictionary again.

Definition of EDIFY from Merriam Webster Dictionary:

1. archaic

a: build

b: establish

2: to instruct and improve especially in moral and religious knowledge : uplift; also: enlighten, inform.

So, as you can see, when you EDIFY your expert correctly, you BUILD them up, you ESTABLISH them as the expert and you UPLIFT them so that your prospect will want to be introduced to them. So, how the flippin' 'eck do you do it?

Here is another formula for you:

FUN

FACTS

FINANCES

HELP

"Amber is a lot of FUN. She knows all the FACTS about this opportunity, she's doing great driving her paid for car (FINANCES) and she loves to HELP people. Hang on, let's see if WE can get her on the line." Piece of cake, just follow the formula.

"He's a lot of FUN, knows all the FACTS about this opportunity, just earned....(FINANCES) and loves to HELP people. Hold on, let's see if we can get him on the line."

What's the most important part of the above two examples? Yep, the "hang on, let's see if WE can get him/her on the line." There's your link into the 3 way call. Please don't ask permission, please don't apologize for trying to get someone else on the line and please don't devalue them with a humdinger of a line such as, "Well, just listen to what they have to say for a couple of minutes then I'll get back on the line." Oh yes, I have heard that one!

Once you have your prospect on hold and you call your expert, brief them on the nature of the call, let them know what 3rd Party Tool your prospect has been exposed to and then ask them how they would like to be introduced. Then complete the 3 way call:

"Hi Jenny, great news, Amber is available! Amber, let me introduce you to Jenny Saunders. Jenny is the lady I mentioned to you yesterday, I am so excited the two of you can get to know each other, over to you Amber."

Then hit mute, get the paper and pen out and make notes! Let the expert be the expert. Under no circumstances do you rejoin the call until invited to by the expert. Listen intently to where the call is going and what the expert is doing and be ready to rejoin the call immediately when you are asked. Remember to listen to exactly what the expert is going to want you to do.

"OK Jenny, great meeting you. I am going to get Paul back on the line and he is going to walk you through the paperwork to get you started. Congratulations, I'll call you tomorrow and we will put together your game plan, well done!"

Or,

"Sounds like this may not be the right time for you to join us, but not to worry. I'll bring Paul back on the line and let's set up a time to get back together in a month. OK, best wishes and let Paul know if you need to speak to me any earlier. Cheers."

Then do exactly as requested, finish off the call and then get back on the line with your expert for a debriefing. Done.

Here's a little quickie to finish this chapter off with. When I am the expert and finish the call, handing it over to the person who set up the call, often I don't hang up, I go on mute instead and listen (OK, sue me!). The most common mistake I hear at this point is the person taking the call back over begins to ramble and throw up on the prospect. This seems to happen most of the time. So, please learn right here right now not to do that. It makes no sense whatsoever. The biggest mistake, bar none, that I hear though is this absolute gem: "So, do you have any more questions?"

Why the *&&^%^ would you ask that question? Nothing good can come out of it and you really have just opened up a can of worms. So, at all costs, DO NOT ASK "DO YOU HAVE ANY MORE QUESTIONS?" when wrapping up the call when your expert has hung up.

Notes

Chapter 15
Mastering Chord 4: How to Ask Them to Join Your Business

Here it is, all the work you have put in so far has led to this phone call, this is the money shot. There is no point plucking up the courage to approach someone on the telephone, piquing interest, exposing them to a 3rd Party Tool, getting them on a 3 way call with an expert and then arriving at the opportunity to call them and sign them up as a customer or a business partner and blowing it. This is where the money is made, so this is the most important call of all. Firstly, as always, you must have a game plan.

- How are you going to start the call?
- How are you going to ask for the order?
- What kind of objections could come swinging your way and how are you going to deal with them?
- What is your strategy for encouraging them to join your business as opposed to just becoming a customer?
- What incentives or promotions are available and how will you use them?
- What are you prepared to do above and beyond the above incentives/promotions?
- Are you going to try and "supersize" the order and if so,

how?

- What is your game plan at the end of the call if they become a customer or a business partner?

- What is your game plan at the end of the call if they don't want to become either?

- Are you going to ask for referrals and if so, how?

- Do you know how to complete the paperwork or online order form? Have you practiced and practiced so that it is second nature?

Lots and lots of questions, but all of them very important and crucial to this being a successful call. Let's get started.

So, recapping our mantra and the title of this book *From Hello to Yes in 3 Minutes or Less* with this telephone call the desired YES is either, "YES, I am ready to join your organization," or "YES, I want to purchase your product and become a customer." Simple.

Now that we have identified our desired YES, we put our game plan together, working backwards to the HELLO, assessing which formulas we may need and when to use THEN SHUT THE HELL UP.

As always, the important thing to do at the beginning of the call is to take their temperature and by now you should know how to do this. Let's recap. It is important to take their temperature right at the beginning of the call so that you know exactly what part of the game plan to move to and it also makes the call more efficient in that you are not going to waste time barking up the wrong tree. Start the call with a nice upbeat, "Hello this is _____ from _____."

And THEN SHUT THE HELL UP.

You will know immediately if they are super hot, ready to get started, or super cold and you have a lot of work to do.

"Oh, thanks for calling. Couldn't sleep last night! We are so excited to be part of this, what happens next?" Is a lot hotter than: "Oh, yes, you know, this isn't for me, when can you come and pick up the samples you left with me?"

If you get the latter response, don't freak out, all isn't necessarily lost. You may just have to ask a couple of questions such as:

"Oh I am sorry to hear that, kind of surprised actually. Haven't heard that sort of response before, may I ask what happened?"

THEN SHUT THE HELL UP.

Let them come up with their prepared response (yes they will have been ready with this) and then once they have stopped talking...

SHUT THE HELL UP.

Let that vein in the middle of your forehead start bulging, but please be disciplined and keep quiet a little longer. Why? Well, what will happen is there will be a little awkward silence, then all of a sudden the person on the other end of the line will start to talk again and reveal the real reason why they believe this is not for them. When they start to talk, do not interrupt, let them spill the beans and make notes of their EXACT WORDS.

Once you think they have really finished, ask them this: "OK, anything else?"

THEN SHUT THE HELL UP.

Often this is the point where the golden nugget is revealed and this is all you need. Once you are convinced that their real objection or concern is now out in the open you can do something about it. I will cover this in Chapter 20.

For now, we will assume that the person on the other end of the telephone is impressed by the product(s) and/or opportunity and is almost there, ready to sign up. At this stage they are just looking for you to exhibit some passion, belief, confidence, and posture. They want you to walk them through the process of what happens next and they almost want you to be responsible for making the decision for them. Exactly how are you going to ask for the order? Please don't use lines like:

"Would you like to sign up today?"

"Would you like me to show you how easily it is to get

started?"

"Have you decided if you would like to join my team?"

"Are you ready?"

Basically avoid questions with a YES/NO answer and avoid questions where you have no idea how they are going to answer. Instead, ASSUME the sale and make it just a matter of fact, piece of cake. Give the impression that you have already done this 5 times today. Also avoid words like "company" or "business" they can be intimidating and sound like "WORK." Instead use "TEAM' or "US." Avoid "Me" or "Mine" or "I."

"OK Jill, all we need to do is figure out where to deliver your starter kit and if you want the regular package or if you really wanted to go for it and start with the premier package. What is your delivery address and when do you want the package to arrive?"

THEN SHUT THE HELL UP.

We have given Jill a few things to think about there and not one of them is if she wants to get started. Instead her mind is focusing on her address and which package to start with and wondering about when that should arrive. As soon as she says, "Well, my home address is..." You get your head down and the ONLY thing you are doing is completing the sign up. No more talking, no more discussing what a great company this is or how pleased you are for her. No mention of training or parties or anything else whatsoever. Your game face is on, your head is down and you are only going to look up once the credit card has been processed and the order confirmed.

Got it?

I am being a little tough on you, but this is go time. This is when the rubber meets the road. I have seen absolute guaranteed sales lost at this crucial time and it is heartbreaking. So please, please, please be disciplined at this moment and follow my advice. Once the order has been completed, put them on hold for a second, let out a sigh of relief and then compose yourself. Get back on the line and carry out the pre planned (remember your game plan?) ending to the call, such as:

"OK, Judy, well done, this is going to be FUN! What happens next is that we need to get together in the next 24 hours and put together your game plan for the next few days. Also, John will be giving you a call, just to check in and help you get off to a fast start. Can you do me a favor? Please don't approach or tell anyone about this yet. It is important that we help you get off to an incredible start and I want you to be fully prepared and ready. Is that fair? Between now and when we get together I am going to send you a video to watch, then just take it easy until tomorrow, we are going to have a blast, but it is important you trust me and let me guide you right from the beginning, OK?"

Let me offer you a few tips regarding writing up the order. Firstly, make sure you know the application upside down and back to front. Practice filling it out many times so that it is second nature to you. This goes for the online version as well. Any doubt or any delay or any mistakes when filling out the application can cause just enough of an opportunity for the prospect to have second thoughts. You want to give the impression that you have done this a million times and it is just a formality.

Next, here is some advice on how to ask for the credit card. Please don't use terms like, "Give me your credit card number," or "I need your credit card information," or "You don't mind giving me your credit card details, do you?" All of the above and any variations on those could be just one final red flag to a prospect as they suddenly realize they are giving their credit card information to someone over the telephone. A much better way and a way I have used thousands of times is this:

"OK, so we accept all major credit cards, go ahead with the number." No need to ask if it is Visa or Mastercard, etc. American Express cards begin with the number 3, Visa cards begin with 4, Mastercards begin with 5 and Discover begin with 6.

THEN SHUT THE HELL UP.

Take down the number, don't forget to ask for the expiration, the 3 digit security code on the back (or 4 digit on the front with American Express) and confirm the billing address. Keep cool, calm and collected and move on to the next part of the application form. That's it!

If your application form requires personal information such as date of birth and social security number, again, these can be sensitive issues and if handled nervously, they can destroy the sale. Here you go, simply use this:

""OK, so what's your date of birth and social?"

THEN SHUT THE HELL UP AND TAKE DOWN THE INFORMATION. Move on to the next part of the application form immediately. Done.

Notes

Chapter 16
How to Supersize the Order

In this chapter I will give you a massive tip and one that will pay back the investment in time and money of reading this book many times over. Most companies will offer at least a couple of ways to become a customer or a partner in their business. For example, your company may have a starter pack of $500 and one at $1000, or another company may offer a $400 and $800 version. Whenever you ask for the order, always ask in a way that the second option presented is the larger of the two. It has been scientifically proven that people are more likely to choose the second option they are presented with. Make sure it goes something like this:

"You can get started today with our success pack at $500 or MOST PEOPLE start with the ultimate pack at $1000, BECAUSE they get much more inventory and some free marketing pieces SO THAT it helps them qualify for the car bonus much much quicker."

Did you notice another one of our formulas there? "MOST PEOPLE...BECAUSE...SO THAT..."

"Most people launch their business with the $800 package, because that helps them get more product out in the market so that they qualify for the free iPad quicker."

THEN SHUT THE HELL UP.

Have some fun with that one, it can literally double your income. Go on, come up with some versions of the formula that apply to your specific opportunity. Discipline yourself to use it every time and practice, practice, practice. Now, this is not going to work every time, but I promise you that over a year, if you present the options in this way every single time and you teach your entire team to do the same, the results will be significant and you can take those results the bank!

Word of caution here: DO NOT MAKE ASSUMPTIONS! Don't tell yourself: *There's no point asking Jenny if she wants to go with the Ultimate Pack, I know she can't afford it.* You will often be pleasantly surprised. Again, once you have wrapped up the order, get off the telephone quickly. I am famous in my regular job for having the "quickest post close close."

"Thank you, well done, good job. I will be in touch when we are getting ready to deliver. Cheers." Then I am off the phone. Nothing else to say really, because if you start to ramble, come across as relieved and grateful for the order, that may just cause a little doubt in your customer. I've seen it happen many times.

Another word of caution: the order may yet need a little work. The saying goes: "People buy on emotion and justify it with logic." So, your prospect will have had emotions running high when they signed up. But very quickly the ether wears off and the logic kicks in. Be prepared for that.

I believe the desired cancellation rate in sales is 7-15%. What the heck do I mean by "desired"? Anyone who boasts that they never get cancellations is not making enough money, I promise you. Why? Because they are not asking for the order enough. If you get 7-15% of your sales cancel, although it sucks when it happens, it means that you are asking for the order, you are completing application forms and you are making more money than someone with a very little or non existent cancellation rate. No need to fight me on this one, just believe me. So, another part of our game plan has to include receiving the telephone call the next day when the buyer's remorse is in full swing. Let's cover this one in the next chapter.

Notes

Chapter 17
How to Handle the Cancellation Call

You just signed up one of your prospects, someone you had been working with for a while and you went to bed last night feeling all warm and fuzzy. Then your phone rings and you see it is your newly signed up business partner calling unexpectedly. Uh oh. Before you pick up the phone, breathe and compose yourself, maybe even let it go to voicemail. In fact, let's let it go to voicemail. Tell yourself that this may well be a buyer's remorse kind of call and you are ready and prepared with your game plan. Here we go.

"Hi Jody, great to hear from you, what's going on?"

They then deliver the telling news that they have slept on their decision, spoke to their spouse and a couple of friends and as a result they feel they made a mistake, rushed into the decision and now want to cancel and get a full refund. No worries, you had a game plan for this right? Here we go:

"Oh Jody, I am sorry to hear that, what happened?"

Yes, you've guessed what you do next. SHUT THE HELL UP. Listen. Make notes. Listen. Let her pour it out. When she has finished, SHUT THE HELL UP again and wait for that now familiar vein on your forehead to start to throb. She may just start to talk again and really open up to the true reason for wanting to cancel. If she doesn't, simply ask her, "I understand Jody, it's natural to have a few concerns. May I ask you, what is the number 1 reason why you feel this way?"

THEN SHUT THE HELL UP. You know the routine.

Now, being the professional that you are, you will have already listed, as part of your game plan, the potential concerns someone might have the day after they sign up. Let's review a few here:

- They don't think they can afford it
- They don't think they are going to have enough time
- They don't think they know enough people
- They don't think they can sell
- They are worried what their friends and relatives might say
- Their spouse is not on board
- An "unexpected" bill just appeared
- They spoke to someone who has done this kind of thing before and they failed
- They have been surfing on the internet and found some bad information about the company and/or the products
- They feel overwhelmed already
- They are nervous
- They feel guilty that they will be taking time and money away from the family
- They don't think they are ready to take on a new challenge

right now

I am sure you can think of some more. Again, you are ready for any and all of the above and your game plan is in place. Let's try this:.

"Thanks for sharing that with me Jody, I appreciate your honesty and I know it couldn't have been easy thinking these things over. I bet you didn't sleep much last night. (She will immediately feel better now and her defenses will drop a little). Just to put you at ease, the company is an honorable and ethical company and they do have a full refund policy. In fact, you have a full 30 days to decide if this is for you, that's great isn't it? (This takes the time pressure and the panic away now that Jody realizes she doesn't have to make this decision right here, right now.) So, why don't we do this, let's meet for coffee, spend some time just reviewing your concerns and maybe even put together a game plan for the next few days. There's no harm in doing that and hopefully once we've met you'll feel a little easier. One of the girls on my team, Kendra, she was in your position, but now she's crushing it. Maybe I can have her give you a call. She could be of help."

The aim of this is to come across again as cool, calm and collected. Let the other person know that this is normal. Tell them a story about someone else who was in the same situation and put them at ease. Again, if this is part of your game plan, when this comes up you will handle it well and more often than not, turn the situation around. Now, there will be the occasional person who digs their heels in and refuses to budge (usually as a result of pressure from someone else). If this is the case, handle it professionally and process the refund. But make sure you end the call on a positive with an agreed upon plan of action. For example:

"So, there you go Jody. I have processed the cancellation and you will see your credit card re-credited in the next few days. Now, before I let you go, why don't I check back in with you in a month and we'll see where you are? Great! Now, if anything exciting comes up before then, do I have your permission to get in touch earlier?"

This sets up an agreed upon follow up, plus an opportunity to call earlier if there is a new product launch or new promotion. Make sure to finish off the call with some more positive news.

"Again, not to worry about all of this, it happens every now and then. I just thought of this though, who is THE ONE person who you know that would be incredible at this? Who is THE ONE person who would jump on this if they knew about it? Thank you, would you mind introducing us, and I tell you what, if she joins the team, I'll let you know and when you are ready, I'll put her in your team to help you get going"

BAM!

Notes

Chapter 18
How to End a Call Correctly, Organize a Follow Up Call and Double or Triple Your Prospects!

If you are wrapping up a call with a prospect and they are not ready to become a customer or join your team, don't beat yourself up and even worse, don't beat your prospect up! Instead, put things into perspective and finish the call with an agreed upon follow up strategy. Why? Well, take a look at these statistics::

According to a study conducted by National Sales Executive Association:

- 2% of sales are made on the 1st contact
- 3% of sales are made on the 2nd contact
- 5% of sales are made on the 3rd contact
- 10% of sales are made on the 4th contact
- 80% of sales are made on the 5th-12th contact

So, even if you have been in touch with your prospect once, followed the system, sent them a third party tool and followed up, that's only two contacts made with the prospect. According to the above stats, only 3% of all sales are made from two contacts or less. So, why would you give up on this prospect with only two contacts made? If you did that with all of your prospects you are leaving 95% of all sales on the table! Instead, finish the call off politely, professionally and with an agreed upon follow up appointment.

"OK John, I understand that maybe right now this opportunity is not for you, no big deal. I hope you have enjoyed learning a little bit about what is on offer and why so many people are recognizing this and joining us. However, sounds like the timing isn't quite right for you. Let's do this, why don't I check back with you in a month or so and see where we are, OK? Great. Now, if between now and then something dramatic shows up on our end like a major announcement or opportunity, should I get back to you immediately? Cool, now before I go, I just thought of something. You're a sharp guy and I have no doubt you hang around with some smart people, who do you think would be the most open person to an amazing opportunity like this? Who do you know who would like an extra 5 paychecks a month coming in?"

THEN SHUT THE HELL UP!

Even when they come up with a name…

SHUT THE HELL UP.

And let them come up with another…maybe two more.

Have you just doubled or tripled your number of prospects?

No really, did I just show you how to completely blow the doors off your business? Go back and read, re-read and assimilate the last couple of sentences. You finished off the call with an agreed upon follow up time, you gained permission to call the prospect earlier (when) needed AND you picked up 1, 2 maybe even 3 referrals! And you also left your prospect with a little seed of doubt in his mind that maybe, just maybe he made a bad decision to turn this opportunity down.

Notes

Chapter 19
How to Follow Up When You Blew It

I am often asked how people can go back to their original list and reapproach people who blew them off in the past. All of us have people who we threw up all over and completely messed up the approach. There's still some diamonds to be mined though in that pile of rubble.

Here's what to do. Write down a list of all the people who you have previously approached and for whatever reason they turned down your offer(s). When writing down the list, do not prejudge them, do not reenact how you went down in flames, do not call a friend to describe just what happened with each and every one of them. Just write the list.

Then, amazingly, and this is clever, start at the top of the list and call the first one. Start with FORM to warm up the conversation and then when you feel the time is right, deliver this beauty:

"Anyway John, you probably remember my botched attempt at introducing my business to you a few months ago..."

THEN SHUT THE HELL UP, LISTEN AND TAKE THEIR TEMPERATURE.

"Well, things have been going well, my team is growing and

developing and it is wonderful to be able to help people develop personally and put an extra 5 paychecks a month into their bank account."

THEN SHUT THE HELL UP, LISTEN AND TAKE THEIR TEMPERATURE.

"I know at the time you stated that this kind of thing wasn't for you, but I was just wondering if anything had changed because we do have an amazing opportunity here for the right person."

THEN SHUT THE HELL UP.

If they blow you off again, refer to the table in the previous chapter to put it into perspective and then schedule another follow up as described earlier in the book. If they do show a change in temperature and they are warmer, be disciplined, have posture, and use the system perfectly.

"Hey, that's cool, I am excited that you are now open to taking a look. If I could drop off a magazine with a dvd inside it, would you take a look and watch it? Great! When will I be able to circle back and pick it up? Because I do have a bunch of other people waiting to get their hands on it."

Another approach for people who you blew it with first time around is to simply call them and just be open and honest.

"Hi Bill, Randy here. I was just thinking about you. Remember when I made a real pig's ear of trying to recruit you for that new business I had just joined? Yeah, pretty dire wasn't it? I am still embarrassed! Anyway, I have been with the company 6 months now and it really has been remarkable how far the company has come since then and of course by now I know what the hell I am doing. Let's get together this week, I have a magazine for you with a dvd inside, we can quickly revisit the opportunity and you never know, this time around I may just be able to show you why these last 6 months have been so amazing. I have been able to help so many people add 5 paychecks a month to their family's budget and I even have people carrying free iPads and driving a brand new car paid for by the company!"

THEN SHUT THE HELL UP.

When Bill starts to talk, keep yourself out of the way and let him open up to you. Keep your discipline, let the conversation go silent, let him then start up again and really reveal the gem you have been waiting for (the real reason he was turned off last time). Then deal with that as normal and schedule the 3rd Party Tool exposure.

Notes

Chapter 20
A Simple Success Formula to Deal With Every Objection You Will Ever Hear

Do you honestly expect to serve an ace every time you play tennis? It would be pretty boring if you did, wouldn't it? Where's the fun in that? Now, every now and then it's great to smash a serve right past the ear hole of your opponent and hear the thud as the ball drives into the back wall of the court. Doesn't happen very often though, does it? So why do you get all disappointed when all your phone calls don't go this way then? Every now and then you'll come across a "lay down" and it makes up for all those nightmares in the past. But really, come on, it just doesn't go like that.

Sticking with tennis, you've served the ball and shock, horror, it wasn't an ace. Do you just stand there rooted to the spot and then when the opponent returns the ball back over the net, you stare at it, crushed that they would have the audacity to do that? Do you look at the opponent and say "Why me? How could you do that to me?" Do you think to yourself: *I bet when Anna serves a ball no one returns it. Everything works out for her.* Do you then quit the game and call a friend and say, "I was playing tennis today, got everything prepared, was wearing my cute new tennis shoes. I warmed up, stretched, hit a few balls and was ready. Then, I served the ball, just liked I'd practiced and you won't believe what happened next. She returned the ball back over the net and won the point."

"What do you mean?" your friend will ask. "Who won the game?"

"I suddenly remembered I had some emails to catch up on. I walked off the court, I'm not playing her again. I am going to try playing someone else tomorrow, but if that sort of thing happens again, I'm done. Maybe tennis isn't for me."

Ridiculous, isn't it? But you know where I am going with this. If you're not ready for the person on the other end of the line to return your service, the game (call) is over. Got it? Let's develop the tennis thing a little further. What kinds of return can she serve back at you? Let's list them:

- a back hand pass
- forehand pass
- a backhand crosscourt
- a forehand crosscourt
- a lob to the net
- a high lob
- a deep return to the baseline
- a short return just over the net

Don't you think you would be a better tennis player if you worked with a coach on how to handle each and every one of the above possible returns of service? Wouldn't you enjoy the game more if your opponent fired one of these back at you and you were ready, dealt with it, and smashed it back at them to win the point? How good would you feel if you played against a really good player, one who really tested you, someone who pushed you and took your game somewhere it had never been before? What if you lost to such a player? Wouldn't you still be a better player as a result? Wouldn't you be more equipped for your next game? Wouldn't you want a rematch at some point? And by the way, how good would you feel if you were clearly the underdog, but due to your hard work, preparation and application, somehow you emerged victorious? Now that's what I am talking about!

Just like the tennis match, let's list the possible returns you'll face from your opponent:

- I am not interested and don't talk to me again about it.
- Oh, I haven't got the time for anything like that.
- We don't have any money to start buying a business right now.
- Did this kind of thing before and it almost cost us our marriage.
- Tracy is dead set against this kind of thing.
- A friend of mine from the gym got involved in one of these pyramid schemes and he still can't get his car in the garage.
- I don't do any kind of business with friends.
- I can't sell, why would you even ask me?

- You're joking right? I can't believe you would try this kind of thing on me.
- I love my career, I'm not going to cheapen what I do by selling stuff out of my garage.
- I don't know anybody.
- I'm not outgoing enough to be chasing down people.
- There's no way I would call any of my friends, I want to keep them!

Ouch! And Bring It On!

We've now established that your job is to serve the ball to your opponent (pique interest) and lo and behold, your opponent is going to attempt to return the ball back over the net for you to deal with (an objection). Rather than write a white paper on all the glorious and sophisticated objection handling techniques handed down since time began (how to overcome "I'm not in the market for a new toga right now thank you" for example) we are going to keep it simple using 3 little words: FEEL, FELT, FOUND. Simple and easy to use.

"I understand how you FEEL. In fact, I FELT the same way, but what I FOUND was..."

Bada Boom Bada Bing.

Let's try it a few times:

"I am not interested and don't talk to me again about it."

"I understand how you FEEL. In fact, I FELT the same way when Jenny called me. But what I FOUND was it's worth at least taking a look at. It probably isn't for you, but worth watching a four minute video just in case, don't you think?"

"Oh, I haven't got the time for anything like that."

"I understand how you FEEL, in fact I FELT the same way, but what I FOUND was once I had rearranged my schedule a little, freeing up a few extra hours a week, I get paid 5 times more per month!"

"We don't have any money to start buying a business right now."

"I understand how you FEEL, in fact I FELT the same way, but what I FOUND was that for less than $500 I could have my own home based business. If you think about it, we spend $200 every time we go to Costco. Joe and I felt it was worth the risk and it's working out, we got all of our money back within 2 weeks!"

"I Did this kind of thing before and it almost cost us our marriage."

"I understand how you FEEL, in fact Sandra and I FELT the same way. What we FOUND though is that this business is a lot of fun and we are enjoying working on something together."

Now, to make this simple formula even more powerful we are going to "Top 'n Tail it." Before you launch into the FEEL, FELT,

FOUND formula, let the prospect really get their objection out of their system and then ask them to describe it a little further, have them explain it to you. I suggest this because oftentimes when a prospect fires an objection across your bow, it is usually a preprepared go to defensive mechanism that doesn't have much thought behind it. Even if you successfully overcome it, it is still rare that you will write up the order.

Why? Because often the real objection is not the first objection they throw at you. The real objection is too personal or too close to them to admit to, so they fire their standard one at you hoping that you are lame enough to not be able to wrestle with it and then they don't need to expose their real concern. So, bear that in mind when their standard objection is delivered, chuckle to yourself knowing that you are now prepared for their little game.

One easy way to deal with this is to simply ask this question: "OK, Joe, let's take the fact that you don't have enough time, off the table. We can work around that. Let's discuss what else is concerning you or holding you back."

THEN SHUT THE HELL UP. AND LISTEN. AND WRITE NOTES.

Wait for the goose to lay the golden egg, the real objection, before you. At that moment, you need patience, you need poise and then develop it further. Have them agitate their own objection. What? Did I really suggest having the prospect describe in more detail their real objection? Have I lost my mind? We want them to describe their objection in detail and then like a jiu jitsu master, we use it on them.

For example, let's say their real objection is lack of money "right now." It's always "right now" by the way! We want them to describe having this objection in the past, having it currently and very likely have it again in the future.

"So Joe, has not having enough money to get started resulted in you missing out on some business opportunities in the past?"

THEN SHUT THE HELL UP and let them describe "the one that got away." Next, ask them this one:

"OK, so what other business opportunities are you currently looking at right now? Do any of those look as good as this one? And do you have the money to start any of them?"

Finally, really stand them up with this belter:

"OK, so in the past you said you missed out on (said missed opportunity) because you didn't have the money. You also described another opportunity you are looking at right now and it sounds like that's not going to happen either. So, let's move forwards 3 years. Let's imagine the opportunity of a lifetime comes up, will you have the money to invest and leap on it then?"

SHUT THE HELL UP.

Let the lightbulb go off. Let them stew on the realization that they have a history of missing out on opportunities in business and unless they make a change, they are likely to miss out on some good ones in the future too. Have them tell themselves, "enough is enough" and decide that they are not going to miss out on this one too.

Now deal with the objection and stick a big fat tail on this donkey by rounding it out with a massive benefit statement like the following:

"Thank you for sharing that with me Joe, I really appreciate it and I understand how you feel. In fact, many of our team felt the same way, but what they found was once they took a look at their finances they managed to come up with the money to invest in their business AND NOW they are paid five times per month, earn a residual income for life and they no longer have difficulty coming up with $500." There is the tail: AND NOW. Work with that, figure out just which AND NOW would work best, pique interest and motivate them to take action.

Here is a summary of the Simple Success Formula:

Let them get their first pre packaged objection off their chest.

Take that one off the table and ask them what else is causing them concern/holding them back.

Then have them discuss that with you and let them agitate it themselves.

Use Past, Present, Future to have them describe this objection in the past, the objection now and admit it will likely be there in the future too.

Then, use FEEL, FELT, FOUND.

Round it off with AND NOW, using an interest piquing/motivating example.

Go through all the possible returns of service or rejections that you are likely to receive and just like in tennis, spend some time preparing for them. This way, when you fire one over the net at your opponent, you are expecting and are ready for a return of service and you now have a simple way of dealing with it. Game, Set and Match!

Notes

_____

_____

_____

_____

_____

_____

_____

_____

_____

_____

_____

_____

_____

_____

_____

_____

_____

_____

_____

_____

_____

_____

_____

Chapter 21
10 Ingredients of a Successful Phone Call Session

Here is a simple list of the key ingredients to set you up to produce a successful phone call session. Just like any successful "recipe" if you leave out any of the required ingredients then the resulting "cake" may not turn out as tasty as you had hoped!

1. Set Expectations and review your WHY.

When you have decided you need to make some more calls to your list, just take a little time to set some expectations and review your WHY. Remember, your whole future financial peace and security does not depend on what happens over the next three phone calls! Review your WHY and spend time really thinking about WHY you have joined your company and what your goals are. Think and write and picture and dream and talk to yourself and imagine and salivate so that you get your game face on for you and your family. Pump yourself up with whatever works for you. Make the expectations of this phone session very reasonable and light hearted such as: *I am going to speak to 6 people from my list, pique their interest and get them in front of a 3rd Party Tool. I'll speak to each of them no more than 3 minutes, thank them for the call and move on to the next one.*

2. Set yourself a reward.

Give yourself a little pat on the back for achieving todays goal. *As soon as I have arranged for 6 people to be exposed to a 3rd Party Tool today, I am going to stop by Starbucks, switch the phone off for 15 minutes and just chill.*

3. Prior Preparation. Ask yourself: *what do I need to review in order to be ready to make the calls?*

- Do you need to review the system and make sure you understand just where these next calls fit in?
- Do you need to review your "script" or at least the components of it such as how you will lead into the reason for the call?
- Do you need to review how you will handle any "objections"?
- Do you need to review how you will introduce your 3rd Party Tool?
- Do you need to review how to schedule the follow up?
- Do you need to review how to get your expert on a three way call, if needed?
- Do you need to review how to end the call if there seems to be no interest at this stage?
- Do you need to review how you will ask for referrals?

4. Practice.

Practice your calls.

Practice how you are going to start the call.

Practice how you are going to pique interest.

Practice some of the reactions you are likely to get and how you will handle them.

Practice how you are going to invite them to your home party. If they won't make the party, what's your back up plan? (e.g. drop off a magazine.)

Practice how you are going to end the call. What's your plan for follow up?

5. Block out distractions.

Log off Facebook, shut down your email, make sure people know you are off limits for the next 30-60 minutes.

6. Block out sufficient time.

No more than 30-60 minutes at a time is needed. Also discipline yourself to 3 minutes per call (use an egg timer).

7. Next!

Be laid back about all of this. If the person on the other line is not up for it and even maybe upset by the call, tell yourself it's their loss and shout out "next" and pick up the phone immediately. Don't think about the call anymore. This is so important, it is hard to put across easily. I have seen people have a "bad" call and it destroys them for the rest of the day. They relive it, replay it, regurgitate it. I have even seen such a call end someone's career!

The important thing here is to get back onto the next call immediately. I know it is hard to do, but it's the most effective way to overcome such a set back. Give yourself 5 seconds after such a call and then pick up the phone.

8. Complete the calls.

If you've decided to call 10 people, call 10 people, simple as that. Remember the reward you have waiting for you! It is so easy to make 2-3 calls and get a mixture of reactions/results, then all of a sudden checking your email sounds like a good idea, or *I wonder what's the latest from my company on Facebook* enters your mind. *Maybe I'll have a coffee, check my list of people, and then make a couple more calls.* Ask yourself: *Will checking emails, going on Facebook, doing some "busy work" in my office move me nearer to or further from my new car?* All the above are natural reactions to the first few calls not going as well as hoped, but letting such thoughts distract you and take you away from the phone is a bad idea. Just keep your head down, maintain your discipline and complete the calls you set out for yourself. One of my old colleagues from years ago used to have a "freshly typed" list of the 10 people he was going to call that day on his desk when he walked in his office. Nothing else was on his desk. All he did each day was call those 10 people. Simple yet dynamite!

9. Schedule your next prospecting calls session.

No matter how the session went, immediately schedule your next. Put it in your diary, on the computer, and in your phone with reminders. Again, it is so easy to put this off until later, especially

133

if the calls did not go as planned. But if you put it off, the week will drift by and all of a sudden you look back and realize that you've spent all of your time doing the fun stuff but you've "forgotten" to call more people on your list. The aim is to schedule the money making activities first and then build all the other stuff around it.

10. Schedule your next follow up call sessions and let your expert know so that they can be ready for any three way calls as needed.

As you will have heard many times: "THE FORTUNE IS IN THE FOLLOW UP." It is perfectly normal to be reluctant on the follow up. You may ask yourself:

What if they didn't like the product?

What if they haven't had time to read the magazine?

What if they feel pressured by me asking them if they....?

Well, they haven't called me, so they obviously aren't interested.

Maybe I'll give them some more time, I don't want to seem pushy.

It was hard enough to get her to try the product, I'll wait for her to call.

These are little stories you tell yourself to justify not making that follow up call. But remember, if you don't follow up as agreed, that indicates to the other person that you weren't serious. This dilutes all the effort you have already put in. Remember, the worst thing they can say is, "I tried it and I didn't like it," or "I didn't read the magazine, I've been too busy and really this kind of thing isn't for me." No biggie, thank them for their time, get your butt over there, pick up the bottle or the magazine and put it in someone else's hands immediately. Once you've completed your phone session, give yourself a pat on the back, enjoy your reward and take solace in the fact that you have just demonstrated The Slight Edge mentality. Now, immediately throw yourself into something else and move on. Well done!

Notes

Chapter 22
Summary and Call to Action

There you have it, *From HELLO To YES in 3 Minutes or LESS*. Let's review to make sure I communicated this mantra to you correctly. *From HELLO to YES in 3 Minutes or LESS* (our second mantra) basically means that before you pick up the telephone to make a call, you decide just what is the desired YES you are aiming for by making the call. The YES could be "YES, I will watch a video." Or, "YES, I will visit your website." Or, "YES, you can drop off a magazine. "YES, I will speak to someone else in your company." Or, "YES, I will attend that hotel meeting with you and YES I am ready to get started. Here's my credit card number."

Once you have determined your desired YES, you then prepare for the call by working backwards through the components of the call all the way back to the start of the call, the HELLO. This is the Game Plan (our first mantra). I described in detail just how powerful the use of silence can be and I described this technique with my third mantra, "THEN SHUT THE HELL UP." Throughout the book I combine this with "Take Their Temperature" which basically means listening to them and gauging just how hot or cold they are at that moment with that topic. Taking their temperature not only helps you decide where to go next with the call, but it can also save you a lot of time, make you more efficient and more effective. I have seen both ends of the spectrum from someone being super cold and then eventually warming up right through to someone being super hot, raring to go and then due to the call being mishandled, becoming suddenly colder and colder and colder until the permafrost eventually kicks in and it is all over.

The pathway from HELLO to YES is made up of not just the use of "THEN SHUT THE HELL UP" but by specific formulas (our 4th mantra) such as FORM, Feel, Felt, Found and "If I COULD...WOULD you...WHEN can I...BECAUSE..."

We then outlined The 4 Chords and worked on perfecting each one. I made the case that if you try to play a well known tune that uses those 4 chords but instead you either play a different chord or omit one completely, then the tune will sound horrible and the results will not be what you want.

My aim for this book is for it to be a working reference book for you, a go to book, a book you carry with you wherever you go when you have your business face on.

I want this book to make you millions.

So, what happens next? Well, Eric Worre said it brilliantly, "It doesn't matter how good YOU are, it's what duplicates." What does he mean by that? Well, here is a fully disclosed plug for this book. It does not matter how much you devour this book, it does not matter how amazing you are at executing all of the techniques in this book. It doesn't matter if, as a result of assimilating the teachings of the book into your very own DNA, you are awarded the Nobel Peace Prize for making the most powerful and effective telephone calls in the history of the world. It doesn't matter how good you are if the rest of your team sucks on the telephone. You want only 1-3% of your income to be as a result of your performance and personal results. The other 97-99% of your earnings should come from the performance of your team.

Now the work begins.

Because if you truly want to leverage your skills and build an empire that is wide and deep, we have shown how important it is that everyone on your team or in your band master the same 4 chords and be able to play sweet music together from anywhere in the world. Why not purchase this book for each member of your team, put a little motivational note in the front and start to build your empire with all of you playing the same beautiful tune.

Notes

Go to www.fromhellotoyesin3minutesorless.com to order the book and follow the instructions to pick up an amazing bonus just for you!

Bonus Chapter 1
Things You Should Always Do

Always assume the sale from the beginning.

Always prepare your presentation with a good beginning, middle and end.

Always ask for the order. Five times if necessary.

Always be ready and prepared for objections.

Always have testimonials and/or third party stories/articles to back you up.

Always have reasons to buy today e.g. pricing, availability, and herd mentality.

Always have a backup plan, such as an additional bonus or discount.

Always ask for the order again immediately after the objection has been overcome.

Always remember that it is no fun if there are no objections. If it was that easy you would be taking orders and be on minimum wage!

Always enjoy the challenge. It's just like an athletic event—if you have prepared well, if you are confident and if you are at the top of your game, you will look forward to the challenge. That is why you are a professional.

Always set an egg timer at the beginning of the call and discipline yourself to end the call within 3 minutes.

Always have a game plan in place before you pick up the telephone. Don't wing it.

Always decide what the desired "YES" is to be and as soon as you receive it, wrap up the telephone call.

Always SHUT THE HELL UP when you ask a good question.

Always listen to your prospect intently and take notes.

Always talk slower than your prospect.

Always talk quieter than your prospect.

Always start each call with taking your prospect's temperature.

Always use "we" or "you" or "they" instead of "I."

Always present them with a second option.

Always use the hold button or mute button if you are getting flustered so that you can regain your composure.

Always shut out distractions when making calls.

Always have your game face on when making calls.

Always treat each call as if you were speaking to the person who could earn you millions.

Always think of a "Columbo" at the end of each call.

Always have an agreed upon action plan at the end of each call.

Always aim to be the best telephone call the prospect has been involved in that day.

Always come back to ask for the order again once you have dealt with an objection.

Always remember, "Facts Tell, Stories Sell."

Always look for positives from each and every call.

Bonus Chapter 2
Things You Should Never Do

Never throw up on a prospect.

Never answer your own prospects questions.

Never mention your company name or its products in your 30 second elevator speech.

Never say what you do or how you do it without explaining why you do what you do first.

Never go into any telephone call without a game plan.

Never pre judge a prospect.

Never use industry terms like "upline" or "downline."

Never ask permission to have someone else join you on the call.

Never ask if they have a couple of minutes.

Never give out a physical 3rd Party Tool without first obtaining contact information and an agreed upon follow up plan.

Never be afraid to use a take away.

Never come across as desperate and grateful that your prospect is even entertaining your approach.

Never apologize for the initial approach.

Never put the telephone down without both parties knowing exactly what will happen next.

Never say goodbye on the telephone without asking for a referral.

Never be afraid to approach someone. You could be the greatest gift they have ever received.

Never forget that the truth is always good enough and therefore never lie about your income, your success to date, etc.

Never forget that this is a netWORK marketing business.

Never forget this is a homeBASED business and not a homeBOUND business.

Never forget that nothing beats Belly to Belly or Ear to Ear.

Never say, "Give me your credit card number."

Never say, "I need your social security number."

Never walk away from an opportunity.

Never regret any unsuccessful approach.

Never take it personally.

Never forget that the general public are nuts.

Never try to understand people.

Never be embarrassed or be ashamed of what you do.

Never forget your WHY.

Never refer to the opportunity as a business, that sounds costly and stressful.

Never interrupt your prospect.

Never talk first.

Never talk more than you listen.

Never criticize another company.

Never say that your company has the best....

Never say that your company has no competition.

Never make claims about your company.

Never look for shortcuts.

Never buy any kind of gizmo or program that promises to take away the need for prospecting for leads.

Never spend more time on social media than on the telephone.

Never forget what the role of a network marketing professional is.

Never put your head on your pillow at the end of the day without having had at least two people ask you what you do for a living.

Never give up on a prospect after 2 approaches.

Never base your entire business on the decisions of a handful of people.

Never stop recruiting.

Never claim you are not selling anything.

Never talk faster than your prospect.

Never talk louder than your prospect.

Never stare at a name on your list and then talk yourself out of calling it.

Never ask Yes/No questions.

Never ask questions when you don't know how they are going to be answered.

Never ask, "Do we have a deal?"

Never ask, "What do I need to get your business today?"

Never come across as desperate for the sale. The prospect will sense it.

Never fumble the writing up of the order. Once you see an opportunity to write up the order, you should be polished and efficient and giving the impression this is the millionth time you have done this.

Never ask, "Would you like me to show you how to get started today?"

Never forget to immediately ask for the order again once you have addressed their objection.

Never go into the presentation without expecting the order.

Never throw the towel in as soon as you receive an objection.

Bonus Chapter 3
Important Formulas for Success

1. To use to build rapport and gather valuable information:

FORM

FAMILY
OCCUPATION
RECREATION
MOTIVATION

"How's the FAMILY? What's going on at WORK? Anything cool going on this WEEKEND? How are you FEELING?"

2. To Pique Interest:

Problem Identify
Problem Agitate
Problem Solve

"Sorry to hear things are tight. What are you doing to get back on track? How long will that take? You know what, I just thought of something, maybe the project I am working on can help."

3. To introduce the use of a 3rd Party Tool:

"Great question _____ and that's why you need to..."

"Great question Susan, and that's why I need to send you an email with a short video to help you understand that."

4. To set up the use of a 3rd Party Tool, button it down, add value to it, and set up the follow up:

"If I could...
Would you...?
When can I...?
Because..."

"If I COULD stop by later today with a magazine, WOULD you take 10 minutes to read it? Great, so WHEN CAN I pick it back up this week, BECAUSE I have a bunch of other people wanting to read it too."

5. To double or triple the number of your prospects when setting up the 3rd Party Tool delivery:

"Who else should WE give one to?"

"I will stop by tonight with a DVD for you to watch, by the way, who else should we give one to?"

6. To introduce the idea of getting an expert on the line for a 3 Way Call:

"Me TOO and that's why we should see if _____ is available, hold on."

"Me TOO and that's why we need to see if Danny is available, hold on."

7. To correctly edify your expert when bringing them on the line for a 3 Way Call:

FUN
FACTS
FINANCES
HELP

"Todd is a FUN guy, he knows all the FACTS about this opportunity, he just earned his $25000 bonus and he loves to HELP people."

8. How to suggest that your prospect should upgrade to the larger starter package:

"Most people start with _____ because _____ so that they can _____."

"Most people start with the Premier Package because it gives them twice as much inventory to start with so that they can qualify for their iPad in half the time."

9. To overcome all objections:

FEEL
FELT
FOUND
AND NOW

"I understand how you FEEL, in fact, many of our team FELT the same way. But what they FOUND was_____ AND NOW they _____."

About the Author

Paul G Walmsley has been a proven expert on the telephone for over 13 years. He has honed and mastered his skills as a commission only salesperson earning multiple six figures a year on the telephone. Paul transferred those skills into the world of network marketing and coaches network marketing professionals on the art and science of using the telephone in their home based business. For more information about this book and the companion workbook *30 Day Business Builder for Network Marketing Professionals: Daily Assignments Workbook,* along with other helpful tools and resources please visit:

www.mytelephonecoachfreeresources.com

Notes

Made in the USA
San Bernardino, CA
01 February 2016